Traditional
Furniture Projects

Traditional Furniture Projects

Percy W. Blandford

TAB BOOKS
Blue Ridge Summit, PA

FIRST EDITION
FIRST PRINTING

© 1992 by **TAB Books**.
TAB Books is a division of McGraw-Hill, Inc.

Library of Congress Cataloging-in-Publication Data

Blandford, Percy W.
    Traditional furniture projects / by Percy W. Blandford.
        p.   cm.
    Includes index.
    ISBN 0-8306-2159-8   ISBN 0-8306-2158-X (pbk.)
    1. Furniture making.   2. Country furniture.   I. Title.
TT194.B543   1991
684.1'042—dc20   91-3057
                                                    CIP

TAB Books offers software for sale. For information and a catalog, please contact TAB Software Department, Blue Ridge Summit, PA 17294-0850.

Acquisitions Editor: Kimberly Tabor
Book Editor: Jack Sherzer
Production: Katherine G. Brown
Book Design: Jaclyn J. Boone
Cover design and photography by Paul Saberin, Chambersburg, PA   HT3

Contents

Introduction   vii

1 Preparations   1

   Planning   3
   Surfaces   3
   Fasteners   4
   Joints   5

2 Seating   11

   Box Bench   11
   Mayflower Stool   15
   Peasant Chair   21
   Library Stool   26
   Rush-Pattern Chair   28
   Wagon Seat Bench   39

3 Containers   41

   Carrying Boxes   41
   Pioneer Chest   47
   Dado Box with Tray   52
   Stacking Bins   55
   Desk   58

4 Hanging furniture   **65**

Hanging Boxes   65
Block of Shelves   72
Hanging Cabinet   77
Shaker-Style Coat Rack   82
Wall Mirror or Picture   86
Hanging Caddy   90

5 Racks and stands   **97**

Quilt or Drying Rack   97
Plant Stand   101
Two-Tier Book Trough   106
Corner Stand   109
Display Rack   113
Turned Stand   118

6 Tables and cabinets   **121**

Slab Table   121
Standard Tables   127
Railed Table   137
Storage Cabinet   141
Small Cabinet   145
Storage Bench   150

7 Utility items   **155**

Carrier/Magazine Rack   155
Drying Frame   159
Steps   162
Rotating Desk Tidy   167
Kitchen Boards   171

8 Outdoor equipment   **179**

Benches   180
Armchair   187
Sawbuck Table   191
Permanent Table with Removable Top   195
Garden Tool Box   198

Index   **203**

Introduction

The term "traditional furniture" is usually assumed to mean furniture made as our forefathers would have done in the not-necessarily-distant past. In particular, we have in mind what are often called Early American or Colonial styles. The emphasis is on solid wood and handwork. Today, this trend is possibly a reaction to the mass-produced furniture made from manufactured boards and in styles that, in some cases, owe more to ease of production than to attractive and functional forms.

Traditional furniture is by definition one-of-a-kind. For this reason, it is suited to the individual craftsman, whether a professional or advanced amateur with an elaborate workshop, or to a beginner with little skill and a few hand tools.

A piece of traditional furniture has its own attraction. It is individual. Other homes will not have identical pieces. Even if you and many others follow a traditional furniture design taken from this book or elsewhere, you will not produce identical items because your craftsmanship stamps what you have made. The added attraction is that you are following tradition. You may make an exact reproduction of an early piece of furniture, or you may make something that follows the earlier style and concept without attempting to form an exact copy. What you will make keeps traditional woodworking craftsmanship alive.

Traditional furniture can have a place in any home, whether town or country—anywhere beauty is seen in furniture that is made to last and designed to satisfy a purpose exceptionally well. It looks fine in a room furnished solely with furniture of similar background, or it can fit comfortably with factory furniture, made mostly of particleboard or plywood. Much of traditional furniture's attraction is the grain pattern in its solid wood construction and its exposed joints.

Making furniture, whether "traditional" or not, takes considerable skill and may be very time-consuming. Judging whether you will be able to find the skill and time for some furniture projects is not always easy. This book attempts to bring together 39 traditional furniture projects that can be completed in one weekend. Obviously, not every person can expect to achieve the same results. However, it is assumed that a weekend means a working time of about 12 hours and that before starting you have what you need, including the prepared wood cut to the sizes given.

What's left are the unknowns of skill and available equipment. If you have an elaborately equipped shop and the skill to use it, you can do much more in a given time than a beginner with a few hand tools and a makeshift bench.

There should be something for everyone among the projects in this book. For a sparsely equipped beginner, a simple project might take the whole weekend, while a well-equipped expert might take all the time he can find to make a more advanced project. Both will achieve satisfaction commensurate with their skills. Remember, a beginner eventually becomes skilled. Do not underestimate your capabilities.

While it would be foolish not to make use of modern machine tools, be careful that you do not spoil the final effect by too obvious evidence of machine work. This applies to surfaces and joints, which are discussed in chapter 1. Do not be put off by size. Complication and difficulty are not related to size. Some big projects in this book are among the easiest.

The book is divided into chapters for convenience, but because some projects are appropriate to more than one chapter, check the book as a whole when looking for a particular type of furniture.

Sizes on drawings and material lists are in inches, unless otherwise marked. Keep to the sizes quoted as closely as possible. Widths and thicknesses are given as finished sizes, but in most cases, a little extra has been allowed on lengths for trimming, cutting joints, and removing flaws.

When making traditional furniture there are a few points and conventions that differ from the making of other furniture. Read chapter 1 to help you adopt the right attitude. It is a guide to making the best use of your weekend. Start on whatever projects appeal to your interests or needs. You will get a tremendous satisfaction out of making traditional furniture, whatever your facilities in skill or equipment.

1

Preparations

Traditional furniture dates from before the Industrial Revolution, when furniture making was 99 percent handwork. That is not much more than a century ago, but we usually think of the products as coming from an earlier age. The important consideration when making furniture in the manner of those early days is the materials they used.

Those pioneers and craftsmen had ample wood at their disposal, in the form of trees that had to be felled and stripped. They used local wood which differed according to the region. Sometimes the wood differed within a piece of furniture, which is one reason why much early furniture was painted. Much of the wood was thicker than we are used to because of the primitive ways of converting logs to boards. Some of the wood might not have been flat. Natural seasoning, the only method they had, takes years. The rule of thumb is one year of seasoning for each inch of thickness.

Many articles were made of only partially seasoned wood, so there was shrinkage and distortion. As things became more settled, sawmills and other facilities developed, available wood became more suitable for furniture, and better pieces were made. These later pieces are typically the ones we want to reproduce.

Only solid wood was used. Veneers weren't used for some time and the usual concept of traditional furniture today does not include veneering. There would not have been a considerable amount of veneering in Europe during the period of fine furniture making. We must also bear in mind that plywood or particleboard didn't exist at the time. Panelling, drawer bottoms, and cabinet backs were problems that were overcome in several ways. Panels in frames were made narrow to suit the widths of available wood, which was cut as thin as possible.

Rear surfaces were often uneven compared with fronts. Drawer bottoms were made with similar pieces across, with dry or glued joints. Cabinet backs might have been made of upright boards with strips over the joints, although tongue-and-groove edge joints were quite early ways of coping with expansion and contraction in boards that covered wide areas.

Glues were not unknown, but they had little strength and did not offer much resistance to dampness, so furniture was constructed to have good mechanical strength without dependence on glue. Furniture makers used fitted and locking joints with wedges. Screws were rare and expensive and were avoided. Usually, nails were used. They were not like the mass-produced round wire nails of today; they were flat, and the head showing on the surface was rectangular or oval. Similar nails are still available today from specialist makers.

You will have to decide what form of traditional furniture you want to make. Do you want an authentic reproduction or something in the style of an earlier piece? If the latter, you must decide if you want to adhere to a pattern or accept materials and techniques only available today.

If you want to make an authentic reproduction, it should be made of local wood and any visible fasteners should look like originals. Joints should be the same as originals and the finish, or lack of it, should be as used by the original maker. There is no reason not to use power tools, but their work should not be obvious, which means doing handwork on surfaces and removing signs of power sawing. Modern glue can be used where its presence will not be evident.

If you want your piece to be traditional furniture style, but not a genuine reproduction, you must decide how far to depart from authenticity. Thin plywood can be used for a carcass back or a drawer bottom, where it is not very obvious. You might use machine-planed wood without trying to disguise it. You might use modern nails or screws, possibly disguised, as suggested later. You could cut joints that depend on their glue rather than the mechanical strength of originals. Using plywood or particleboard structurally, however, would be taking things too far for the piece to be called traditional furniture. If you use solid wood and combine modern methods of construction with older designs, you may satisfy yourself it is traditional furniture, but there are limits—such as a traditional furniture television cabinet!

In the earliest days there was very little hardware for furniture, so wood was used for fasteners and hinges. Some hardware was smith-made, but most of this was more appropriate to larger work. Hinges were imported or made locally, and these were more often surface-mounted than let into edges. Reproductions of hinges and other hardware are available, and you will have to decide whether to use these or allow a modern type. Fortunately, where only the knuckle of a hinge shows, it does not detract from an otherwise authentic appearance.

Door and lid fasteners were often omitted, or a wooden turnbutton was used. If you are not trying to be too authentic, it makes sense to use an inconspicuous modern spring or magnetic fastener. Much early hardware was iron, but brass and other metals arrived and you would be correct to use them.

Planning

To get the most out of your available time, you need to know what you have to do and plan ahead. Make sure everything is ready, down to things like drill bits, nails, and screws. Most of the wood should already be cut to the right sections. If you have to take time out to visit a lumberyard or a hardware store, your production schedule will suffer.

Study the instructions and drawings. Make sure you know what to do and in what order. Usually it is unwise to try to cut corners. Do all you can to every piece of wood while it is an individual item. Working on a strip of wood on a bench is easier than trying to do things to it after it is built into other parts. Sometimes you have to delay drilling a hole or cutting a notch until after partial assembly, but if you can prefabricate a piece of wood before doing anything else with it you will save time and might improve accuracy.

Make sure parts that should match really do. If there are four legs or similar parts, put them together and mark the positions of joints and other positions common to all of them (FIG. 6-7), even is some will need additional marking. Watch squareness throughout. You cannot get squareness if at some subassembly stage you do not check the particular parts.

Surfaces

You won't be felling trees and converting logs to boards. Instead, you will be starting with wood that is machine-planed, or you will put it through your jointer. This is your first obstacle to authenticity. Even if we accept surfaces that are more parallel than if done by hand, we will have areas that do not look right, unless the piece of traditional furniture is not expected to be very authentic.

Machine planing leaves the surface with a series of ripples or ridges across the grain. In good-quality planing, with a slow feed, this may not be very obvious, but it will show through a finish. Pounding is a less-obvious effect. Blunt cutters—all cutters are less than perfectly sharp after the first cut—compress as well as cut the surface, which may cause general unevenness or uncut fiber ends that will rise. If not dealt with, this effect later becomes more evidence of machine planing.

Sanding, particularly power sanding, is not the complete answer if you want to produce a surface like an original. It will improve a surface and you may find it acceptable, but there was very little sanding on early furniture. Ideally, the surface should be hand-planed to remove machine plane marks. If the characteristic uneven slight hollows or handwork are left, they may be regarded as authentic touches.

Scraping the surface is another method. You can use a modern scraper, or you can remove a plane blade and use that as a scraper, as many earlier cabinetmakers did.

Dampening the surface and letting it dry is a further step. This should lift any bent fiber ends and allow you to scrape them off. The original furniture maker probably would have left it at that. If he considered sanding, it really was sand. Dry sand, with a wood block to provide pressure, would have produced a final surface something like modern sanding. Power sanding is too drastic, but you can lightly hand sand with a modern abrasive paper wrapped around a block of wood.

Fasteners

For a reasonably authentic nailed assembly reproduction you should get cut nails made to earlier patterns. Several versions are available, but most are comparatively large, making them less suitable for smaller furniture. Cut nails (FIG. 1-1) tend to be thick in relation to their size. You should drill the holes for them, even well away from ends, to minimize the risk of splitting. Drill undersize in the lower wood and almost full-size in the top piece.

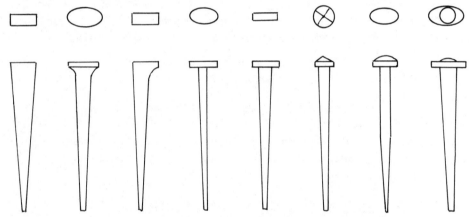

Fig. 1-1. Types of traditional nails.

You might prefer the convenience of modern nails. If punched below the surface and covered with stopping, the construction might not be quite as traditional, but it may be an acceptable technique, particularly if the surface will be painted. You can increase strength in nailed joints by using glue and then driving nails in a dovetail fashion, with closer nails in open corners (FIG. 3-1).

Modern screwheads don't differ much from early screws, but too many screwheads visible on a surface are no more attractive now than they have ever been. Screws with round heads were not unknown, but showing too many round head screws might not be authentic.

Screws have an advantage over nails in their ability to pull parts together. Even if you use glue in a nailed joint, hitting at one place may loosen another. Screws are preferable. Modern techniques of counterboring and plugging were not used in early furniture, but you will probably find them acceptable. You need a plug cutter, so you can cut cross-grained plugs from scrap wood similar to that used for the furniture. This determines the size holes you drill. Counterbore to suit the plug, then drill for the screw in the usual way (FIG. 1-2A) and glue in the plug (FIG. 1-2B) with its grain the same direction as the surrounding surface grain. Plane and scrape the plug level with the surface and it should not appear very obvious.

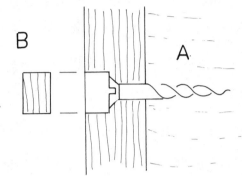

Fig. 1-2. Plugging a counterbored screw.

Joints

In much early furniture joints were exposed and obvious to any viewer—a tenon would go through, dovetails went through both ways, and other joint details were there for all to see. You should strive to maintain this characteristic of traditional furniture. You must also remember that some joints we are familiar with were not in use. These are mostly the products of the machine age.

Although the use of dowels goes far back into history, using them for joints where they are the main members, as practiced today, was unknown. In the past, dowels were made by knocking a roughly shaped short piece of wood through a hole in a steel plate. These dowels were used to reinforce other joints or for their security. Fortunately, modern dowel joints can be used in many situations as they will not be seen on the surfaces, and no one will be able to tell. Exceptions are where the viewer would expect to see tenons showing through or some other place where an exposed part of a different type of joint would have been seen.

Half-lap, or halving, joints were commonly used and are easy to cut by hand. The common halving joint (FIG. 1-3A), crossing squarely or at another angle, may have both surfaces level, but it requires so much to be cut from each piece that the joint is weakened. More strength is retained if the parts can be crossed without surfaces matching and by making shallower notches (FIG. 1-3B). This is seen in the crossing legs of many sawbuck tables.

The dado joint was probably called by the British name of housing joint by the early users. There are plenty of examples of its simplest form (FIG. 1-3C). The

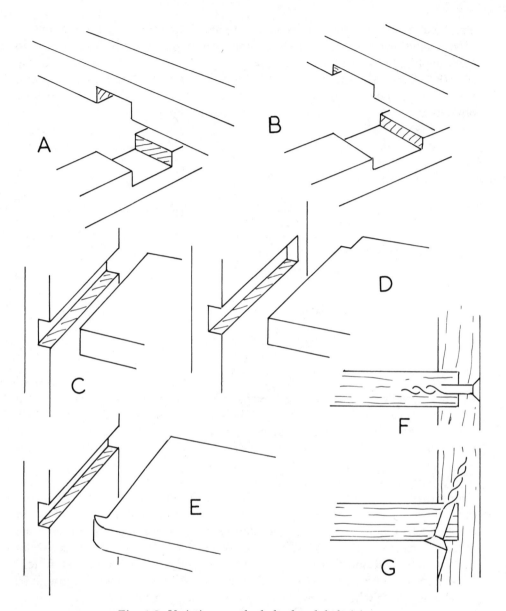

Fig. 1-3. Variations on the halved and dado joints.

stopped version, which makes a neater front to shelves (FIG. 1-3D), is not so easy to cut. Letting the shelf project and overlapping the end of a through groove is an alternative (FIG. 1-3E).

Even with modern glues, a problem with a dado joint, is that all the meeting surfaces have end grain against side grain, and glue does not grip well on end grain. Nails or screws can be taken through from outside (FIG. 1-3F), but if you want to avoid metal heads showing on the surface, you can drive the nails or screws diagonally upwards from below (FIG. 1-3G). If the assembly has a back, it may strengthen these joints. Then you need only nail or screw near front edges, one in each shelf or just in top and bottom ones. More details of dado joints are shown in FIG. 4-7.

The mortise and tenon (FIG. 1-4A) is the commonest structural joint found in much early furniture. We are inclined to use dowels instead of tenons in some places, but mortise and tenon joints are usually stronger and are necessary in much traditional furniture. Usually the tenon is made one-third the thickness of the mortised piece. Tenons are sometimes secured with wedges outside the tenons (FIG. 1-4B). It is stronger to spread the tenon, instead of compress it, by driving a wedge into a sawcut across the tenon (FIG. 1-4C). In a wide tenon, there could be two wedges. Always spread in the direction of the grain of the mortised piece. In the past, this provided mechanical strength, but today you may wish to use glue as well.

For multiple tenons, such as where the leg is tenoned to a stool top, the wedges might be placed at alternate angles to form a pattern (FIG. 1-4D). An interesting hidden version of locking a tenon is called "foxtail" wedging. A tenon with one or two sawcuts across is called a stub tenon. The mortise is undercut at slight angles to allow the tenon to spread, then short thick wedges are put in the sawcuts before the tenon is driven home (FIG. 1-4E). You have to estimate the size of a wedge and the amount of spread it will produce.

"Draw pinning" was a common way of tightening a mortise and tenon joint in sizes ranging from those in house frames to those in the smallest furniture. This was used to secure joints when no satisfactory glues were available, and it is still a worthwhile method even if glue is also used.

Cut the parts of a normal mortise and tenon joint, then drill across the mortised part for a dowel (FIG. 1-4F). Mark and drill a hole in the tenon slightly nearer the shoulder, so when the joint is assembled the two holes are out of line (FIG. 1-4G). Prepare a dowel twice as long as the thickness of the mortised piece to fit the hole. Point one end, no farther than halfway (FIG. 1-4H), and drive it in. The tapered end will pull against the misaligned holes and draw the tenon in. Drive until all the round part is through, then cut off the ends. In some house structures the draw pin was square, but in furniture, make it round. There are many variations of the mortise and tenon joint. Some of these are described where they occur in projects.

Early furniture makers were proud of their dovetails. They did not have the help of jigs or mechanical cutters, and the joints were made completely by hand. Although dovetails produced by using many modern dovetailing guides may be good, they do not produce dovetails with similar proportions to those in traditional handmade furniture. For authenticity, it is better to lay out dovetails more like those made by early craftsmen, even if this means mostly handwork.

The side of a dovetail should be close to an angle of 1 in 7 (FIG. 1-5A). The width of a tail should not normally be more than twice the thickness of the wood (FIG. 1-5B) and the pins between might be one-fourth of this (FIG. 1-5C). While

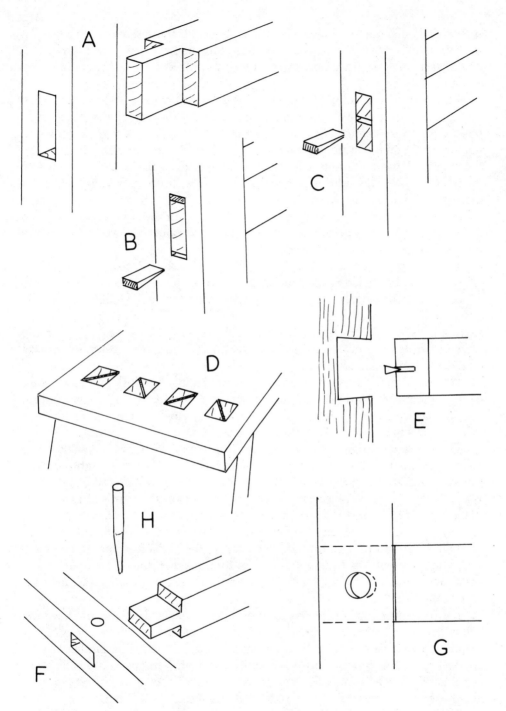

Fig. 1-4. Methods of securing mortise and tenon joints.

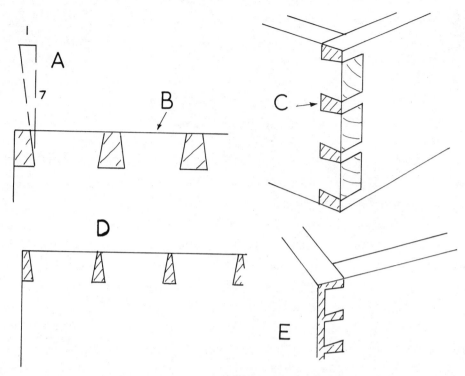

Fig. 1-5. *Details of traditional dovetail joints.*

some early cabinetmakers were very proud of their skill in cutting joints with very narrow pins (FIG. 1-5D), this could not have been as strong, but it still appears to be strong enough and you might wish to emulate their skill.

Drawer fronts (FIG. 1-5E) are the only places a half-blind, or stopped, dovetail joint would have been used. The same rules for spacing apply, and the effect is like a normal through dovetail with a narrow piece of solid wood ahead of it. Some variations of the dovetail joint are described where they occur in projects.

2
Seating

We all need something to sit on, and some of the earliest furniture makers produced various forms of seating among their first products. Seating has developed so that the making of modern chairs is a fairly complex process, and the reproduction of such a piece of furniture could not be regarded as a weekend project. Much seating of years gone by would also be too complex to reproduce in a weekend. However, many simple seating ideas from the past have uses today and are worth making.

Chests for storage were usually of a height suitable for sitting on and formed some of the first supports for those who tired of standing. If you make a chest, you might consider sizing it about 16 inches high, so it can double as a seat. As an alternative, you might make a shallower chest with legs, so a bench seat is also a storage box.

Some of the more basic chairs from Early American and Colonial days might form traditional furniture projects, and most can be made in one weekend. Such substantial furniture will stand up to harder use than your better modern chairs and could be made for a family room, a club or games room, or for your workshop. If you furnish a room with an Early American or other historical theme, well-made stools, benches, and chairs will enhance their surroundings.

Box Bench

Some early benches were long because this was the easiest way to accommodate large families and because boards converted from logs tended to be large, and the makers wished to avoid the heavy hand labor of reducing the wood to make lighter furniture. You might make a large bench for use outside or in a clubroom, but a smaller version would be more appropriate to a modern living room.

A bench made in the same way as an earlier one, but smaller, could also include storage. This bench (FIG. 2-1) is fairly compact, but it is at a suitable height for sitting. The top lifts to expose box fitted with one or more trays. The trays could house needlework, knitting or weaving materials, or you might store your hobby equipment inside. The bench can be used at a piano or keyboard to store music. You also can add a lock to the box, so the contents are secure against pilfering.

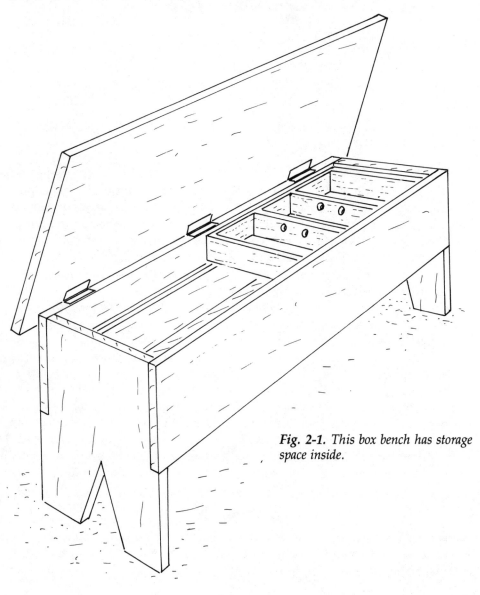

Fig. 2-1. This box bench has storage space inside.

A local hardwood is the most suitable material. To use in a living room it should be sanded and given a polished finish. Elsewhere it might be left with a less-advanced degree of finish. If you want the bench to appear old, you can distress and round edges and surfaces unevenly to give a semblance of wear.

Materials List for Box Bench

2 legs	1 ×	10	×	17
2 sides	1 ×	9	×	34
1 bottom	1 ×	8	×	32
1 top	1 ×	12	×	38
2 tray supports	$1/2$ ×	$1/2$	×	32
2 tray sides	$1/2$ ×	$2^3/4$	×	17
2 tray ends	$1/2$ ×	$2^3/4$	×	10
2 tray divisions	$1/2$ ×	$2^3/4$	×	9
1 tray bottom	$1/4$ ×	8	×	16

You can amend sizes to suit available wood. An early bench would have been made with boards of the full width. You might have to glue pieces together. Cut nails would make joints similar to those of early benches. You might use dowels, without exposing them on the surface. Screws with exposed heads would not be appropriate. You might use screws with their heads counterbored and covered with cross-grained plugs. All methods are described in the instructions. If you do not wish to make too authentic a reproduction, you could use plywood for the bottoms of the box and trays.

1. Mark out the two legs (FIG. 2-2A and B). Cut recesses for the boards that will be used for the sides. Make V cuts to form feet.
2. Cut a piece for the bottom to fit between the sides (FIG. 2-2C). Make the sides to fit in the recesses in the legs (FIG. 2-2D).
3. If you intend to join the parts with cut nails (FIG. 2-3A), drill the outer pieces to prevent splitting. You might have to make undersize holes in the lower part if the wood is very hard. Spacing the nails about $1^1/2$ inches apart should be satisfactory.
4. If you want to dowel the parts (FIG. 2-3B), drill all pieces at the spacing suggested for nails. Dowels $3/8$-inch diameter will be suitable. Drill as deeply as possible in the outer pieces, without the drill breaking through. Prepare sufficient dowels, and glue the whole assembly in one operation.
5. If you intend to use counterbored screws (FIG. 2-3C), drill and counterbore equally in the outer pieces. Glue and screw the sides to the legs. Then fit the bottom between the sides and glue and screw it through the sides and the legs. Glue in plugs and plane them level after the glue has set.
6. Level the top edges, if necessary.
7. Make the top overlap 1 inch at the sides and 2 inches at the ends. Take the sharpness off all edges and lightly round the corners.

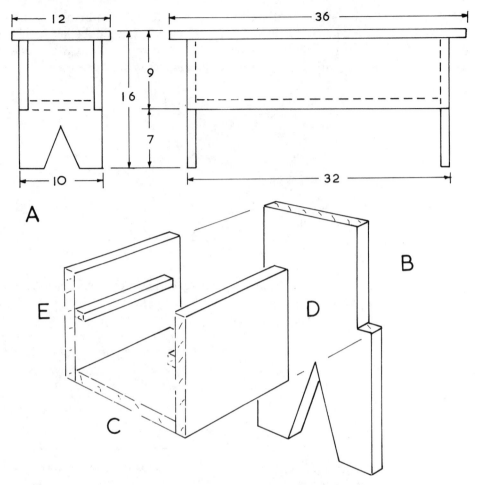

Fig. 2-2. *Sizes and assembly details of the box bench.*

8. Use three 3-inch stout hinges under the top, with one 6 inches from each end and the third at the center. Screw to the surface of the top, but let the leaf of each hinge into the edge of the side (FIG. 2-3D). Let the hinge in sufficiently for the top to close down easily.

9. You could put a hasp and staple at the center of the opening side if you want to secure the box with a padlock.

10. The box bench is complete, unless you want to fit one or more trays. Trays may rest and slide on supports on the box sides (FIG. 2-2E). You might make one tray to slide along and give access to things below without lifting it out, or you might make two or more trays to fill the space above the supports, then lift them out to open the lower part. Much depends on your requirements.

11. A suitable tray would be half the length of the box and wide enough to

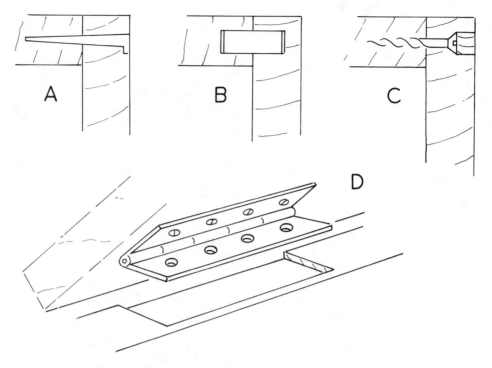

Fig. 2-3. Corner joints and hinge details for the box bench.

slide easily on the supports (FIG. 2-4A). This one is shown with two divisions, but you can arrange the tray to suit your needs.

12. Make the tray as a light box. You can simply nail the corners, but it would be stronger to notch them so nails might be driven both ways (FIG. 2-4B). The best joints would be dovetails (FIG. 2-4C). Divisions can be fitted into grooves or just nailed in. Finger holes in the divisions will help in lifting out a tray. Make the bottom of the box of thin wood or plywood. Arrange the supporting runners inside the main box at a height that keeps the top edge of the tray 1/4 inch down from the top of the sides.

Mayflower Stool

A stool that is not too low to sit on, but also can be used as a footrest and a step stool has obvious uses in any home. This stool is of that size (FIG. 2-5) and incorporates a small drawer. Its name comes from the original association with the Pilgrim ship *Mayflower* and with Plymouth, Massachusetts.

Legs are flared both ways, improving appearance and stability. If anything is given considerable double flare, the angles of edges are affected but with this moderate flaring, edges can be cut square at first and lightly beveled where necessary during assembly. Parts can be nailed or joined by any of the methods described for the box bench.

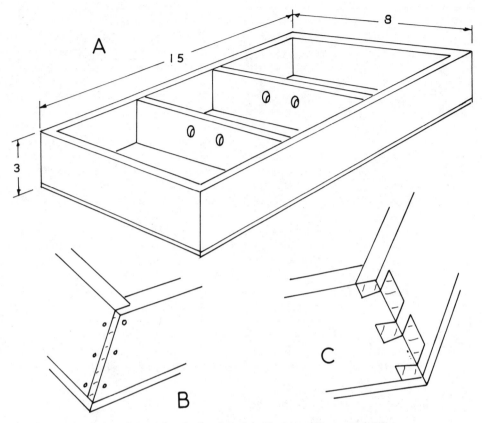

Fig. 2-4. Tray for the box bench and alternative corner joints.

Except for the drawer, which should be made from thinner wood, all parts can be 3/4 inch thick. Ideally, you should use a local hardwood, but you can use softwood. Early stools were untreated or painted, but if you use an attractive hardwood and plan to use the stool in the living room, a clear finish would look good.

Materials List for Mayflower Stool

2 legs	3/4 ×	12	×	16
2 sides	3/4 ×	7	×	19
2 drawer supports	3/4 ×	5	×	12
4 drawer guides	3/4 ×	3/4	×	12
2 drawer sides	1/2 ×	31/2	×	12
1 drawer front	1/2 ×	31/2	×	10
1 drawer front	1/2 ×	31/2	×	11
1 drawer back	1/2 ×	3	×	10
1 drawer bottom	1/4 ×	8	×	12

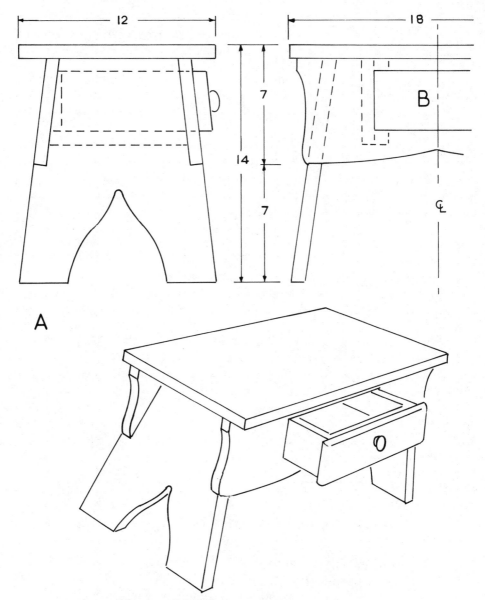

Fig. 2-5. A Mayflower stool includes a drawer.

1. Obtain the angle of the endwise slopes by drawing the main outline of an end (FIG. 2-6A).
2. Mark out and cut the two legs (FIGS. 2-5A and 6B). Your angle drawing will show you the bevels to cut the top, bottom and notch surfaces (FIG. 2-7A). Make the notches to suit the wood to be used for the sides.

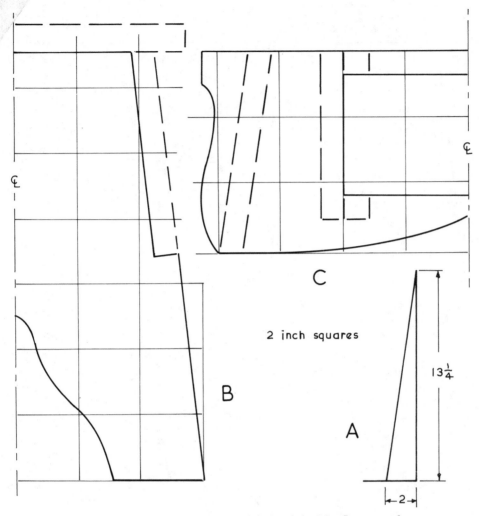

Fig. 2-6. *Shapes and layout of parts of the Mayflower stool.*

3. Mark out and cut the outlines of the two sides (FIGS. 2-6C and 7B). Mark the drawer opening (FIG. 2-5B) in one piece, but do not cut it yet. Mark where the two drawer supports will come on the inside of both pieces.
4. Put the two sides in the notches of the legs and clamp them there temporarily. Measure inside the sizes and angles of the drawer supports (FIG. 2-7C). Cut these pieces and fit the drawer guides to top and bottom edges.
5. Compare the drawer supports and guides with the marked drawer opening in one side piece. Cut the opening so that when the drawer is entered, the cut edges are in line with the guides.
6. Assemble all parts. See that the top edges come level and the drawer supports are fitted squarely and parallel.

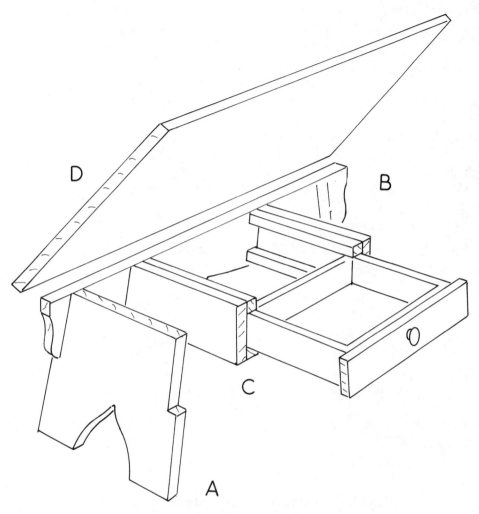

D

B

C

A

Fig. 2-7. Assembly details of the Mayflower stool.

7. Make the top (FIG. 2-7D). Mark on it the location of the other parts and prepare it for joining on, but leave the assembly open until after the drawer has been made and fitted, so you can check its action and make any needed adjustments while you can see the inside of the framework.
8. The drawer is a box sliding in the stool, with a front extending on each side to act as stops. The traditional construction would be with a solid wood base fitted in grooves and dovetails at the corners, but you may choose to use a simpler construction with a plywood bottom. Both methods are described.
9. The rear of the drawer will be upright, but the front has to match the slope of the cut side. Cut a piece of wood which will form one side and mark it to serve as a guide in the construction of the drawer (FIG. 2-8A).

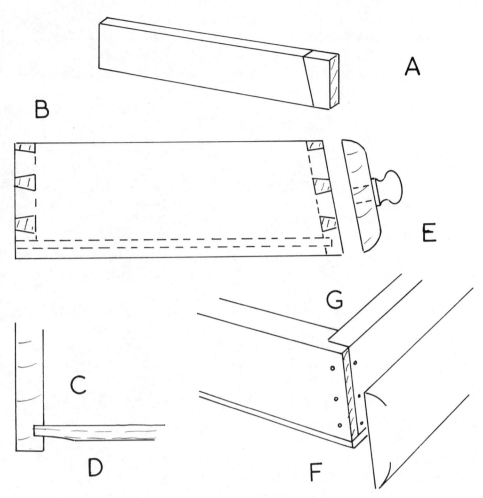

Fig. 2-8. Details of the drawer for the Mayflower stool.

10. If you use dovetail drawer construction, mark out a pair of sides (FIG. 2-8B). Allow for the bottom fitting into grooves (FIG. 2-8C) and mark the dovetails to allow for this. The back goes above the bottom in the side grooves.

11. Mark the sloping front with pins to match the side dovetails and groove the wood to match the sides.

12. Cut the joints. Have the wood for the bottom ready. It might be thicker than the widths of the grooves, so its underside can be reduced to suit (FIG. 2-8D).

13. Assemble the drawer parts. Pull the joints tight and slide in the bottom from the rear. Screw it upwards into the back. Plane the joints level after the glue has set. Test the fit in the stool.

14. Make the false front the same depth as the drawer, but let it extend ¹/₂

inch on each side (FIG. 2-8E and F). Round all front edges. Fit a central knob. Join the false front to the drawer with glue and screws from inside.

15. You can make a simpler drawer as a box with a plywood bottom. Cut the sides to shape (FIG. 2-8A) and notch them to take the crosswise parts (FIG. 2-8G).

16. Make and fit the back and front. Join them to the sides with nails driven in from both directions. Glue and nail on a thin plywood bottom.

17. Level all edges and try the drawer in the stool.

18. Add a false front similar to that described for the dovetailed drawer.

19. Join on the stool top. In an original stool, the top would have been nailed on, with the nail heads exposed. You can punch the nails below the surface and cover the heads with stopping or use dowels or counterbored screws.

20. Remove all sharp edges and sand thoroughly before applying your chosen finish.

Peasant Chair

In many parts of Europe, notably Germany, Austria, and Switzerland, a type of chair favored in many households was made like a four-legged stool with a substantial back, all cut from thick wood. The back often was decorated elaborately. This type of peasant chair was also made by immigrants from these countries. The Pennsylvania Dutch (actually *Deutsch*, meaning German) made these chairs. With the more urgent need for completion, the backs may have been less elaborately decorated. As most wood was converted into fairly thick boards, these chairs could be made without further reduction in sections.

This peasant chair (FIG. 2-9) is made of close-grained hardwood, 1¹/₄-inch finished thickness. Softwood is unsuitable.

Materials List
for Peasant Chair

1 seat	1¹/₄ × 16	× 20	
1 back	1¹/₄ × 16	× 24	
4 legs	1¹/₄ ×	1³/₄ × 22	

The chair can only be made strong enough by using mortise-and-tenon joints. Do not try to substitute dowels. The chair is a test of your ability to cut mortise-and-tenon joints at angles other than 90° to the surface. Original chairs were made of single boards of the full width, but you may have to glue together narrower pieces.

1. Prepare wood for the seat and the back, with parallel edges and marked centerlines. Leave a little extra on the length of the seat (FIG. 2-10A) and allow plenty of extra length for the tenons on the back (FIG. 2-10B).

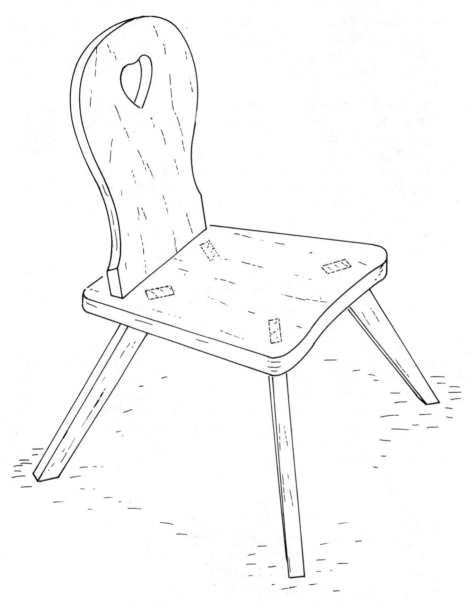

Fig. 2-9. This peasant chair has stout parts tenoned together.

2. Mark out the shape of the seat (FIG. 2-11A), but leave shaping the outline until after joints have been cut. Mark the positions of the mortises on the top surface. At the front they are on lines at 45° to the corner. At the back they are on lines at 30° to the corner. They will be ³/₄ inch wide, but you will only know the exact lengths after tenons have been cut on the legs.

3. Mark out the shape of the back (FIG. 2-12A). Some originals were much more elaborate and you may wish to use a different outline. Heart cutouts

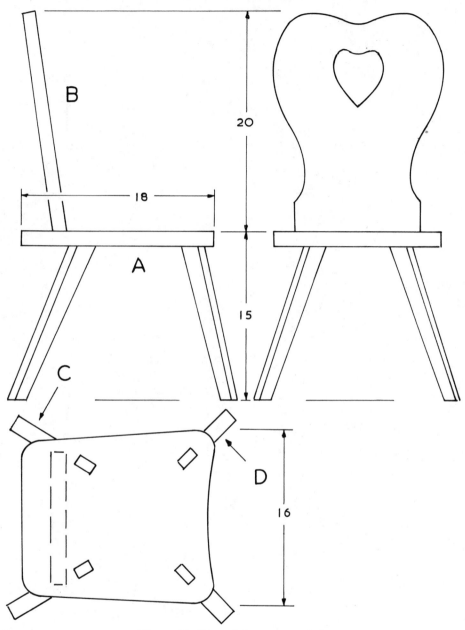

Fig. 2-10. Sizes of the peasant chair.

were popular. This cutout is also a hand grip for lifting the chair. Leave shaping until after the tenons have been cut. Mark the tenons on the front surface. They and the spaces between them are 1 inch wide. Some extra length goes through the seat and is levelled afterwards. Do not cut the tenons yet.

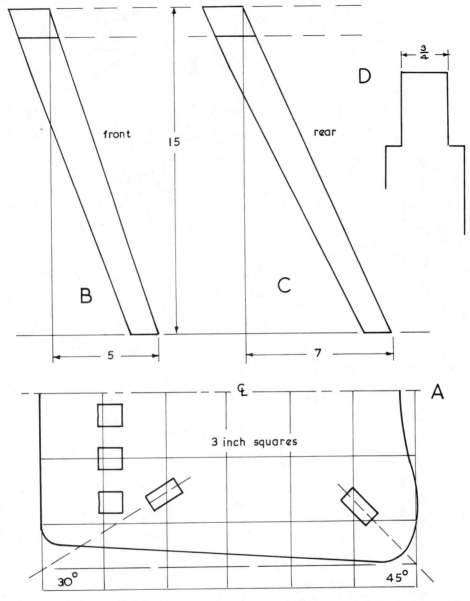

Fig. 2-11. Shapes and layout of parts of the peasant chair.

4. The exact angle of the back in relation to the seat is not critical, but it should be between 5° and 10° to vertical. If you allow for its top edge to be positioned vertically above the back of the seat, that will be satisfactory. Try this position and set an adjustable bevel to the angle.
5. Mark the angle on the edges of the back at the base of the tenons and draw across the rear surface. Cut the tenons.

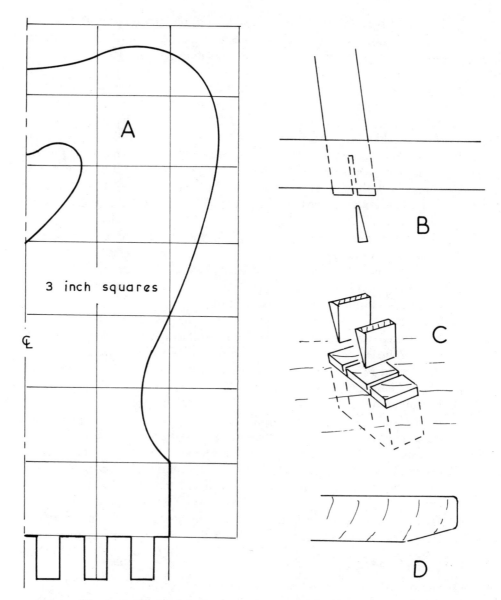

A

3 inch squares

₵

B

C

D

Fig. 2-12. Shape of the back and joint details for the peasant chair.

6. Check that the spacing of the mortises on the seat match the tenons. Mark the angle on the edges of the seat board and square across on the underside. With these top and bottom lines as guides, cut the mortises. Much of the waste can be removed by drilling at the correct angle, but you will have to finish the mortises by hand with chisels.
7. When marking out the legs, consider them as viewed from their sides (FIG. 2-10C and D). Set out full-size the angles of the legs (FIG. 2-11B and C).

Leave the legs the full width of 1³/₄ inch while marking out the tenons. Mark the angles of the shoulders, allow enough length to go through the seat, with a little left for trimming, and mark the tenons ³/₄ inch thick (FIG. 2-11D). Cut the tenons.

8. Leave the legs the full 1³/₄-inch width to 3 inches below the seat, then taper the inside edges to 1¹/₄ inch square at the foot. Leave trimming the bottom of each leg until after the assembly, as it is unlikely the legs will stand level at the first setting.

9. Using your preliminary markings of the mortises and tenons as guides, mark the actual sizes to be cut on the top of the seat. At the rear leg positions, check that the leg mortises will be clear of those cut for the chair back. If necessary, move the leg mortises forward to provide enough clearance.

10. With the leg tenon angles as guides, cut the mortises through the seat.

11. Make saw cuts across all tenons for wedging. Cut so tightening will be in the direction of the grain, allowing for single wedges in the back tenons (FIG. 2-12B) and two wedges in each leg (FIG. 2-12C). Trim tenons so they will project through no more than ¹/₈ inch.

12. Complete the shaping of all parts, including taking off sharpness and smoothing edges. Smooth around the heart cutout. Round the front and sides of the top of the seat. Legs should be left angular at the top, but may be tapered to a more rounded section at the feet. Seat edges may be thinned a little (FIG. 2-12D).

13. Assemble in two stages, starting with joining the back to the seat. Glue the joint and draw the parts tightly together, then drive in wedges. When the glue has set, level the wedges and projecting tenon ends.

14. Add the legs a pair at a time. Sight across to see that angles are the same before driving in wedges. When fitting the second pair, sight along as well as across. Slight differences in angles are not important. When the glue has set, level the wedges and projecting tenon ends.

15. Try the chair on a flat surface. Check that the height of the seat is the same all around. If necessary, take a little off the bottom of one or more legs. When you are satisfied with the level, round all bottom edges of the legs so they will not mark the floor covering.

16. Some early chairs were brightly painted and you can finish in this way if you wish, but, if you have used a good hardwood, the chair will look better with a clear finish. Avoid too high a gloss.

Library Stool

In the library of a large house, one of these stools was used for reaching higher shelves. The extended leg formed a handle for carrying the stool and for steadying the person using the stool. Most of us do not have libraries with books on high shelves, but in many places in the kitchen, and elsewhere, cabinets and shelves are out of reach from the floor. The extra 10 inches that this stool (FIG. 2-13A) gives makes all the difference. The stool will also serve as a seat, not only for a child, but when you want to work on or near the floor, without actually sitting at that level.

For regular indoor use as part of the home furniture, the stool ought to be made of a hardwood and given a good finish. If you want to use softwood and

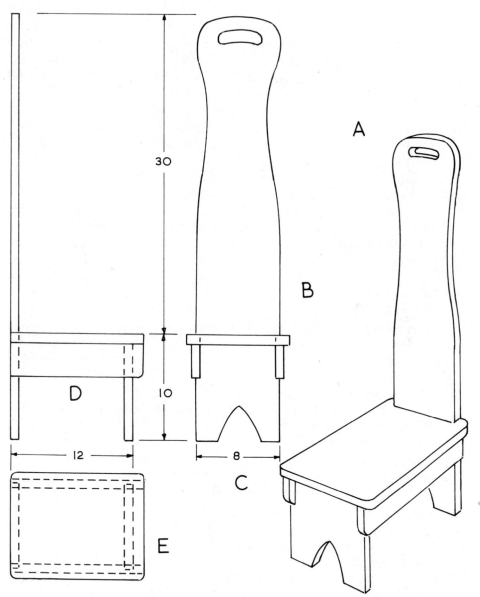

Fig. 2-13. A library stool has a long handle for steadying yourself.

paint it, increase thicknesses by 1/8 inch. You can use dowels, but the strongest construction will be with counterbored and plugged screws.

Materials List
for Library Stool

1 long leg	3/4 ×	8 ×	42
1 short leg	3/4 ×	8 ×	12
2 sides	3/4 ×	3 ×	15
1 top	3/4 ×	10 ×	15

1. Make the leg extended to form a handle (FIG. 2-13B). Cut the notches at the sides 3/8 inch deep (FIG. 2-14A) and high enough to take the sides and the top (FIG. 2-14B). Shape the bottom cutout to form feet.
2. At the top of this piece, mark a hand hole and shaped outline (FIG. 2-14C). Round the edges of the hole and the outside parts that will be gripped. You might round the lower parts of the shaping or leave the edges square and merely take sharpness off them.
3. Make the short leg (FIG. 2-13C). Cut it to a shape to match the other leg, but stop it under the top.
4. The two sides (FIGS. 2-13D and 14D) finish level with the edge of the long leg, but extend 1 inch past the short leg, with rounded bottom corners.
5. The top (FIGS. 2-13E and 14E) is 1 inch wider than the legs. It is level with the outside of the long leg and extends to the ends of the sides 1 inch outside the short leg. Cut its end to fit into the long leg notches above the sides.
6. Drill the holes for counterbored screws. Arrange two holes at each crossing of the sides over the legs and others at about 3-inch intervals through the top and from the rear leg into the top.
7. Round the exposed edges and corners of the top. Round or take sharpness off other exposed parts.
8. Glue and screw the sides to the legs and cover the screw heads with glued plugs. Allow the glue to set and plane the plugs level before adding the top.
9. Apply your chosen finish. Avoid a high-gloss finish on the top, which might make it slippery.

Rush-Pattern Chair

There is usually a need about the home for at least one strong side chair. Modern, lightly-built chairs are surprisingly strong, but they may not survive rocking without the joints weakening or parts breaking. This chair (FIG. 2-15) follows the earlier, more substantial designs used by traditional craftsmen. One of these chairs might be made for the kitchen, at a table used for a hobby or wherever a single chair is needed. You might make a set to go with a traditional-style table.

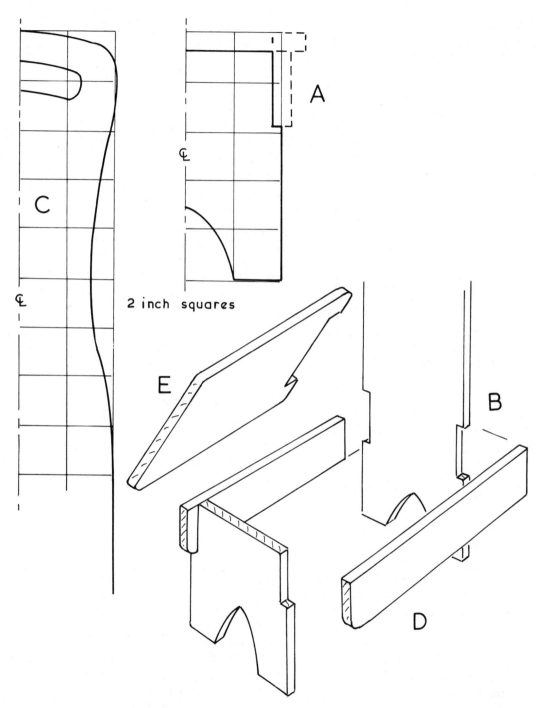

C

A

℄

2 inch squares

℄

E

B

D

Fig. 2-14. Shapes and assembly details for the library stool.

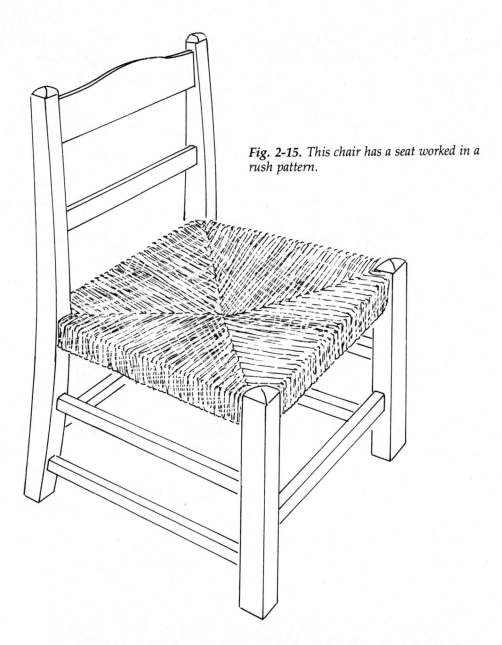

Fig. 2-15. This chair has a seat worked in a rush pattern.

Early chairs were seated with rush from the riverside that was twisted wet into a rope form as it was worked. If you can find suitable rush and are prepared for the rather messy and tedious work this method is still possible, but it is more convenient today to use a prepared cord. Several types are available but seagrass gives an effect nearest to natural rush and is available in its natural grey/green color, or dyed—which would not be appropriate to this chair. The instructions assume you will use seagrass.

You should make the chair framework from one hardwood, preferably a local one, for the traditional effect. Softwood is inappropriate because it is not strong enough in the joints, unless the sections are thickened to the point that the chair would look clumsy and ugly. Most joints described in the drawings and instructions are mortise and tenon. This follows original practice. Although using dowels in some joints might be possible, at least two in each place would be needed and this is impossible with some wood sections. All joints in a chair should be close-fitting and wedges may be needed for any that are not as tight as you wish. Use strong waterproof glue, preferably a two-part boatbuilding type, for maximum strength.

The suggested sizes (FIG. 2-16) are for a normal dining room chair. The seat area should suit most users. You might reduce sizes to make a child's chair, or increase the height to use at a bar counter. Compare the suggested sizes with other chairs you have, then decide on any variations you wish to make.

It should be possible to make the chair framework in one weekend if you have all the material ready cut to correct sections. The framework should be partially finished before you work on the seat and then you should apply the final coat. If you make the framework during a weekend, weaving the seat will provide a few hours of work for another time.

If you make a set of chairs, you should make them together, preparing parts for all the chairs at the same time. That will give you a more exact match and you will also save time, although the number of weeekends will be almost the same as the number of chairs. Prefabricating the parts involves a minimum of change in adjustment of equipment, whether you have a fully mechanized shop or are doing all the work by hand.

Materials List
for Rush-Pattern Chair

2 rear legs	$1^1/2$ × 3	× 34	
2 front legs	$1^1/2$ × $1^1/2$	× 18	
4 seat rails	1 × 2	× 17	
6 lower rails	1 × 1	× 17	
1 back rail	$5/8$ × 4	× 17	
1 back rail	$5/8$ × 2	× 17	

1. Start with the two rear legs because the sizes of several other parts have to match them. Use a $1^1/2$-inch by 3-inch section of wood. After shaping, the ends will be $1^1/2$ inch square.
2. Mark the seat position (FIG. 2-17A). Leave the wood parallel for about 1 inch above and below the seat rail location, then curve to $1^1/2$ inch wide at the ends. The best way to do this is by springing a lath to shape and drawing along it.
3. Mark a width of 2 inches at the seat position. Draw curves from the mark to the ends.

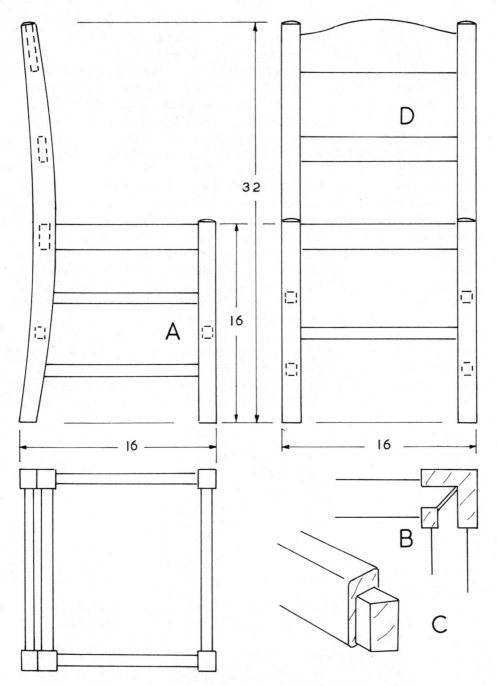

Fig. 2-16. Sizes of the framework of the rush-pattern chair.

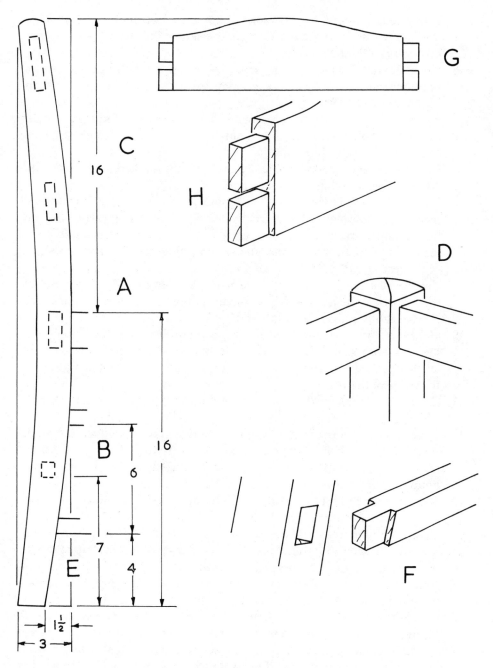

Fig. 2-17. Rear leg details and structural arrangements of the rush-pattern chair.

4. Mark the layout with the positions of the lower rails (FIG. 2-17B), drawing the lines across for those that come at the side of the chair. Mark the chair back rail positions (FIG. 2-17C).

5. Using the rear legs as a guide, mark the wood for the front legs, so rail positions match (FIG. 2-16A). Leave some extra length at the tops for shaping later (FIG. 2-17D).

6. Before cutting the rear legs to shape, note the extra lengths and angles that must be allowed for the lower side rails (FIG. 2-17E) because of the leg curve.

7. Cut the rear legs to shape. Make sure both are marked for joints to the other pieces, and that they are paired.

8. Prepare the wood for the rails. All tenons are $1/2$ inch wide. The seat rail tenons enter the legs until they meet with miters (FIG. 2-16B). The other rail tenons do not meet in joints, so they can be cut square to enter about $3/4$ inch. Cut the bottom side rails with sloping shoulders to match the shape of the rear legs (FIG. 2-17F).

9. Cut the seat rails. Tenons into the rear legs may be full-height, but cut them down at the front so the end-grain in the legs is not weakened (FIG. 2-16C). Lightly round the edges of the rails.

10. Make the crosswise lower rails the same length between the shoulders as the crosswise seat rails. Use the side rails as a guide for marking the lengths of the lower side rails, leaving the extra you have noted to match the curve of the rear legs.

11. Cut all the tenons you have marked and make the mortises in the legs to take them.

12. Since the two back rails are thinner, you may have to reduce the tenon thickness to $3/8$ inch. Draw a shaped edge to reduce the top rail from 4 inches to 3 inches (FIG. 2-17G). Mark and cut double tenons (FIG. 2-17H). Round the rail edges.

13. The other back rail (FIG. 2-16D) is straight and parallel. Round its edges.

14. Cut mortises for the rails in the legs.

15. Make sure all mortises are deep enough to allow the tenons to fully enter. Take the sharpness off the edges of legs and lower rails and shape the tops of all legs. They can be beveled, but they will look best if curved (FIG. 2-17D). Leave at least $1/4$ inch above the rails on the front legs before curving, to allow for the thickness of the seating.

16. If all the joints are cut correctly and fit tightly, then glue is all that is needed for assembly. If a joint needs reinforcing, you might put a wedge inside in a saw cut or a pin or thin screw driven across a tenon from inside, where the head would be inconspicuous. You could also use this as a means of holding joints close while the glue sets, if you do not have enough clamps.

17. Join the pairs of legs with the crosswise rails first. The parts should pull together squarely, but compare diagonal measurements to make sure

there is no twist. Put the front assembly over the rear legs and make sure the legs and rails are in the same positions. You should let the glue dry on these assemblies before joining them with the other rails.

18. Join the side rails to the front assembly first. Check squareness and then add the rear assembly. Stand the chair on a flat surface and see that it stands with the front legs upright. Before the glue has set, check squareness as viewed from above and compare the diagonals at seat level. You may also need to make a similar check at foot level, but you should be able to see if there is any twist by looking through the seat frame.

19. Remove surplus glue and finish sanding. At least partially finish the wood before working the seat. Stain the wood and apply one or two coats of clear finish. If you fully finish at this stage there is a risk that you might damage the surface when handling the chair while working the seat pattern, so you should apply the final coat of finish later.

20. Natural seagrass is the recommended seat material. Its color is similar to rush and can be bought by weight in hanks already twisted into cord. If you have a choice of thickness, thicker is preferable for this chair. Thinner cord requires more turns and may look neater on a stool, but seagrass 1/4-inch diameter looks more like rush.

21. Two tools, which you can make, are needed for the seat pattern. One or more shuttles are needed for winding the cord. The shuttles can be crude and made from scraps of wood 3/8 inch thick and about the suggested size (FIG. 2-18A). Toward the end of the pattern you need a wooden needle (FIG. 2-18B), preferably straight-grained hardwood.

    Drill two holes slightly bigger than the seagrass at one end and taper the other end to a point. Wood about 1/4 inch by 1/2 inch is suitable. You can put as much line as possible onto a shuttle or only moderately fill it, because the knots in the seagrass will be hidden, so the number of joins do not matter.

22. Knot the end of cord hanging from the shuttle and tack it to the inside of a chair rail (FIG. 2-18C). Take the line over the next rail, around the top of the leg and back over the first rail (FIG. 2-18D). That is the entire action you have to master. Repeat that action until the entire seat is covered.

23. Pull the turns tight at that corner and hold onto the tension while you go to the next corner and do the same there (FIG. 2-18E). Keep the tension as you move to the next corner. An assistant is helpful to have so one of you can hold a corner tight while the other makes the turns at the next corner.

24. When you get around to the first corner, put the new turns inside the first. Continue around in this way. As you progress, keep the turns pressed tight along the rails and make sure the pattern forms reasonably squarely to the rails. You will see the pattern underneath is the same as on top and the lines from corner to corner come inside, where they will be hidden. When you join in a new cord, tie the knot in a line between corners.

25. This seat is not square. As you get near to filling the side rails change to a

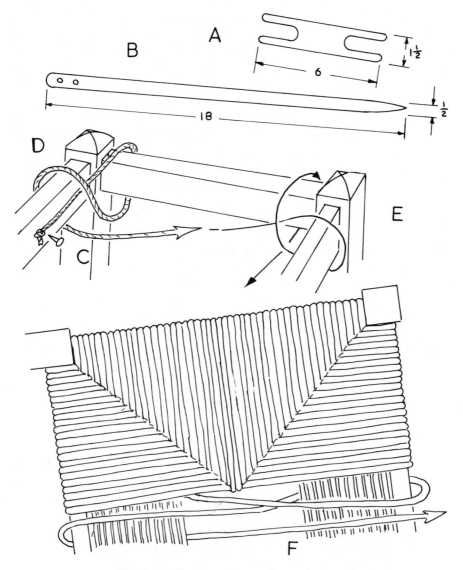

Fig. 2-18. How to work a rush-pattern seat.

needle because there will not be enough space at the center to pass a loaded shuttle. Push an end of the line through one hole and then the other. Friction will hold it.

26. Pack the side rails with turns as closely as possible, then change to a figure-eight action (FIG. 2-18F) to fill the pattern in the other direction. Press turns close along the rails and use the point of the needle to force open the hole in the pattern at the center until you cannot put on any more turns. Finally, tack the line under a rail and push the end into the pattern.

27. Give the woodwork its final coat of polish or other finish.

Wagon Seat Bench

A bench for two takes up less space than two separate seats. Early woodworkers made some benches more comfortable by fitting backs and ends. A common source of ideas for the design was the wagon seat, and many benches were completed with a family likeness to the seat on a wagon. A seat for two made this way (FIG. 2-19) has an old-world charm and might be used on a porch as well as in a living room. The sizes given (FIG. 2-20A) are for a substantial piece of furniture, as it would have been when first made, but you can lighten sections of wood a little, particularly if a strong hardwood is used.

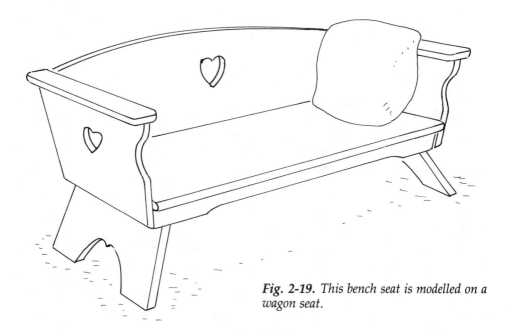

Fig. 2-19. This bench seat is modelled on a wagon seat.

Early wagon seat benches might have been nailed, but you can make a more attractive piece of furniture by using counterbored screws with cross-grained plugs over the heads. For 1¹/₄-inch wood, the screws could be #10 or 12 gauge by 2¹/₂ inches. For some parts you could use ⁵/₈-inch dowels. Make the bench with wood having planed surfaces, but for an authentic, traditional look you should remove all signs of machine planing.

The wagon bench seat is best built in stages. First, make and assemble the bench part, and then attach the ends and the back. The legs, end and back all slope and you need to ascertain the angles before cutting wood. Draw a line representing the top of the seat and another crossing it squarely. Measure heights on this and the amounts of slope of the end and leg (FIG. 2-20B). Do the same for the slope of the back (FIG. 2-20C). Use these angles when making the relevant parts, setting saw guides or marking the angles with an adjustable bevel.

Materials List
for Wagon Seat Bench

2 bench sides	$1^{1/4}$ ×	4	× 52
2 legs	$1^{1/4}$ ×	18	× 18
1 seat	$1^{1/4}$ ×	19	× 52
2 ends	1 ×	13	× 21
1 back	1 ×	16	× 56
2 armrests	1 ×	4	× 22
2 strips	$1^{1/4}$ ×	$1^{1/4}$	× 18

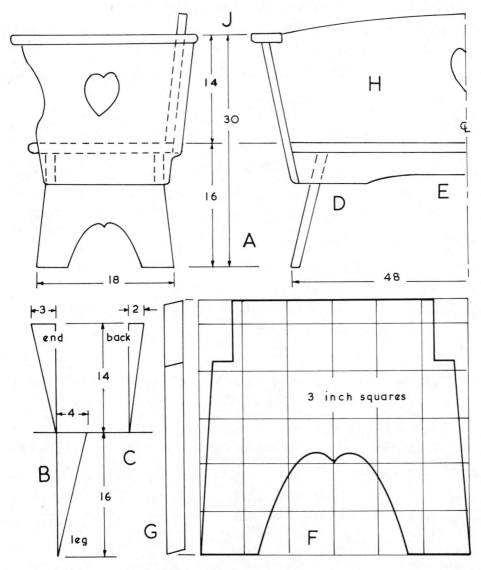

Fig. 2-20. Details of the wagon seat bench.

1. Draw the two bench sides (FIG. 2-20D). Mark the positions of the legs, and slope the ends to suit the angle of the bench ends. You might reduce the depth of the central part of the front rail to 3 inches and round its edges for comfort in handling.
2. Set out the two legs (FIG. 2-20F). Bevel the notches and the ends (FIG. 2-20G). Make sure the notches fit the actual depths of the sides. The bottom shaping should complement the hearts cut in the ends and back.
3. Join the legs to the sides. Secure each position with glue and three screws.
4. Mark the board for the bench seat. You may have to glue boards together to make the seat wide enough. At the back, the seat edge overhangs the frame sides by 1 inch and is beveled to suit the slope of the back. At the ends, the edge should continue the slope of the frame sides. At the front, the edge should project 2 inches over the frame side and be rounded (FIG. 2-21A).
5. Attach the seat to its underframing, using screws at about 6 inch intervals.
6. Check the angles and make sure the edges are level where they have to meet bench ends and back.
7. Mark the pair of ends (FIG. 2-21B). The rear edge extends past the back of the seat, so a strengthening strip can join each end to the back (FIG. 2-21C). Bevel the top edge so the armrest will be level after assembly (FIG. 2-21D). Hollow the front edge of the bench end and round its section. Round the outer edge of the bench end where it will overlap the bench sides. Make the heart cutout large enough so you can use it as a handle to lift the bench. Round the edges of the heart so the edges aren't sharp.
8. Glue and screw the strengthening strips to the rear edges of the bench ends, then glue and screw the ends to the bench seat and sides.
9. Using the assembly as a guide, make the back to fit (FIG. 2-20H). Bevel the back's lower edge to fit on the seat. Bevel the ends so the back fits neatly inside the strenghtening strips at the ends. The top edge can be straight, but a moderate curve looks better. Leave curving until you can fit the edge to the armrests. Make a cutout at the center the same size and shape as those in the ends for decoration and lifting.
10. Make two armrests (FIG. 2-20J) to extend past the strengthening strips and 1 inch forward at the front. Round all edges and corners.
11. Cut away the ends of the back so it fits under the armrests and complete shaping the top edge.
12. Join the back to the seat with dowels or secure it with screws drilled upward through the seat. Use counterbored screws at the ends into the strengthening piece and drive more screws through the bench ends into the back, to produce strong corners. Fit the armrests with counterbored and plugged screws.
13. Blend overlapping parts into each other by rounding edges and corners. Stand the feet on a flat surface to make sure it doesn't wobble. Trim if nec-

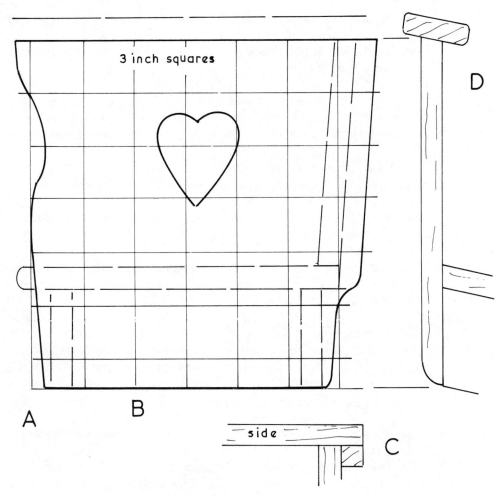

3 inch squares

A   B   side   C   D

Fig. 2-21. *Details of the end of a wagon seat bench.*

essary, then bevel the feet lightly all around to reduce the risk of splintering or marking the floor.

14. Finish to suit the wood and situation. Softwood might be painted, as were many early examples. If you have used a good hardwood, it will look better stained and given a clear finish.

3

Containers

If things are to be kept together for convenience and tidiness, we need containers. Some of these may be cabinets and cupboards, which are dealt with in chapter 6. This chapter covers boxes and chests, which are usually portable.

Many settlers arrived with their possessions in chests, which had to serve as their first furniture—both as seats and as storage. Reproducing these chests is an interesting shop project, and the chests can be attractive as well as useful pieces of furniture. A blanket chest is a typical adaption of an early settler's chest, but other chests may be in many different sizes and patterns.

Small containers can be purely utilitarian or beautiful as well as useful. You can put a lot of work into carving, inlaying or otherwise decorating a small container, without using much wood. Most small containers are primarily functional and it is these that will occupy your time in a weekend workshop.

A container's size does not necessarily affect the amount of work involved in making it. Shaping and joining large boards may be no more complicated than making a much smaller box. The small container could include more exact work, if it has cut joints, while the large chest is most likely nailed or screwed.

Carrying Boxes

There are plenty of uses for boxes that can be carried about and several patterns from earlier days still have uses. Boxes vary from quite small ones with a single handle to others that require two hands or even two people. Construction may be simple nailing or more elaborate cut joints.

The wood might be almost anything available, and you will have to judge the suitability of wood for the purpose of the box. A gardening box may be made of a combination of softwood. A box for your living room would be better made from furniture-quality hardwood and given a finish in keeping with the furniture in the room. If the box will be used for food, the wood should be free from resin or oil. For tools or anything heavy, consider the strength of the wood.

For simple boxes the bottom is nailed to the sides. This puts the weight of any load directly against holding the bottom (FIG. 3-1A). Nails are better able to resist weight if they are driven at alternate dovetail angles (FIG. 3-1B). It is better to have the bottom within the sides, either in one direction or both ways (FIG. 3-1C).

If the sides are nailed together the grip is in probably weak end grain. Use nails of ample length at dovetail angles. If the top of the box will be open, put two nails close together at each top corner (FIG. 3-1D). To reduce the risk of splitting, drill the top piece the same size as the nail, particularly near edges. You may need to drill undersize holes in the lower piece if it is very hard wood or the nails are large.

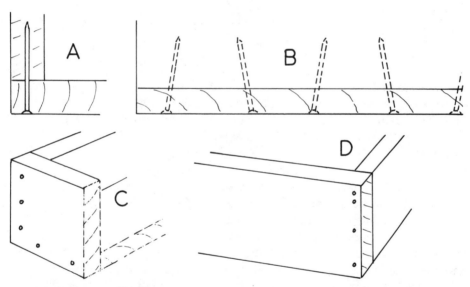

Fig. 3-1. The use of nails in constructing a box.

Screws are stronger than nails, and can be either countersunk level or counterbored and covered with plugs. Much depends on the quality of finished work you require. Cut and glued joints will be better than nails or screws. Some examples are shown in the following design details.

A simple nailed box might have raised ends to form handles. Simple handles are made by attaching a strip on the outside (FIG. 3-2A) to form a finger grip. A better handle can be made by cutting through (FIG. 3-2B). Make the hand hole 1-inch by 4-inch minimum. A better hole to standardize on is $1^{1}/_{4}$ inch by 5 inch (FIG. 3-2C), unless space is very restricted. You can drill the ends and saw away the waste (FIG. 3-2D) and smooth and round the edges.

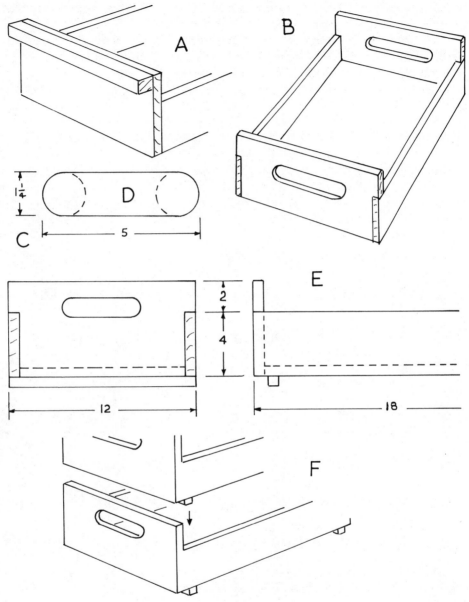

Fig. 3-2. Designs for stacking boxes.

The suggested sizes for a box (FIG. 3-2E) will suit garden seed boxes, carrying canned food or any oddments. You can make boxes of any size by the same method.

Strips going across the bottom serve two purposes. They act as feet and you can use them for locating if you stack several identical boxes (FIG. 3-2F). If the boxes are not expected to be in regular use and you want to store two or three compactly you could arrange them to nest, if you make the boxes in reduced sizes to fit easily into each other.

That type of box needs two hands for lifting. Many occasions call for a box with a central handle (FIG. 3-3A). You can carry tools in it. It will bring cutlery to the dining table. It will hold sewing or knitting requirements.

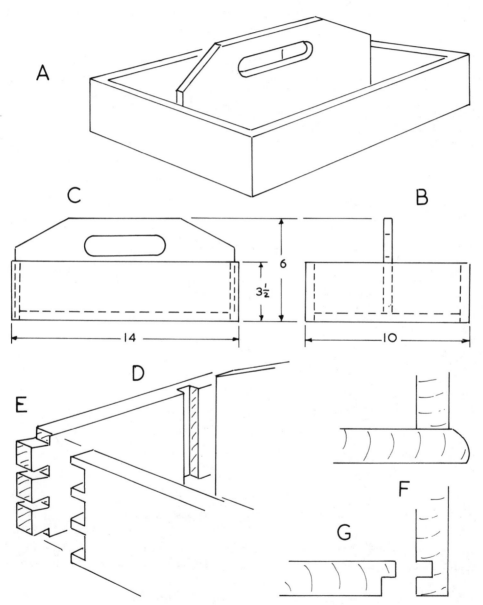

Fig. 3-3. Construction of a box with a central handle.

The sizes suggested (FIG. 3-3B) should suit most of these uses. For basic purposes all the parts can be nailed. The central division should be made high enough so the hand hole is clear of the contents (FIG. 3-3C).

For a better quality box, the divison should fit into dado grooves (FIG. 3-3D) and the corners could be dovetailed (FIG. 3-3E). For cutlery or other light load you can put the bottom underneath with a rounded overhang (FIG. 3-3F) and attach the other parts with glue and screws. If the bottom is to go inside and you want to avoid nail or screw heads showing on the outside, groove the sides for a tongue on the bottom to fit in (FIG. 3-3G). Such a box in a good hardwood with a clear finish and exposed dovetails will serve as an example of your woodworking craftsmanship.

To carry heavier loads, a box based on the old dough box might be suitable. After dough for bread was mixed and kneaded it was left to rise before being formed into loaves and baked. This type of box was used both to store flour and to hold the dough while it rose. Box sizes vary from those large enough to be permanently located to smaller ones that could be put on a table. In between were boxes as illustrated here (FIG. 3-4A).

The sizes suggested would carry a heavy load and should not occupy too much room and can be carried by two people (FIG. 3-4B). These boxes are always made with either the ends or the sides flared. The bottom fits inside the ends. Handles are rods between the sides.

Materials List
for Carrying Boxes

First box			
2 sides	$5/8 \times$	4	$\times$ 20
2 ends	$5/8 \times$	6	$\times$ 14
1 bottom	$5/8 \times$	11	$\times$ 19
Second box			
2 sides	$1/2 \times$	$3^{1}/2 \times$	16
2 ends	$1/2 \times$	$3^{1}/2 \times$	12
1 bottom	$1/2 \times$	9	$\times$ 15
1 handle	$1/2 \times$	6	$\times$ 16
Third box			
2 sides	1 $\times$	12	$\times$ 32
2 ends	1 $\times$	12	$\times$ 13
1 bottom	1 $\times$	10	$\times$ 20
2 handles	$1^{1}/2 \times$	$1^{1}/2 \times$	14

1. Mark out the pair of sides (FIG. 3-4C) with shaped ends (FIG. 3-5A). You can cut angular ends, but shaping will improve the appearance. Mark the centers for the handles, but do not make any holes yet.
2. Locate the ends (FIG. 3-4D) in slots (FIG. 3-4E). The slots are mainly for positioning and to prevent movement. Keep the slots shallow—$3/16$ inch deep in 1 inch boards is sufficient. The ends are shown level with the sides at

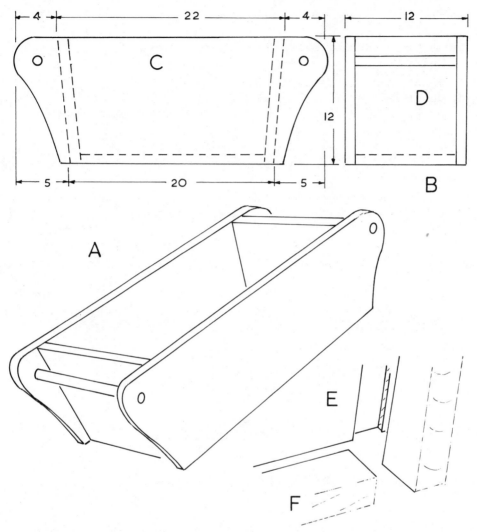

Fig. 3-4. A box with handles at both ends.

the top, but you can extend them up with rounded edges, if you wish. Cut the bottom (FIG. 3-4F) to fit inside.

3. Original dough boxes had handles made from square sectioned wood, with the corners taken off. If you choose these handles, cut tenons on the ends (FIG. 3-5B) and make mortises in the sides to suit. It would be a little stronger to stop the chamfers (FIG. 3-5C), which is easy to do with a suitable router cutter.

Round handles are more comfortable. You can use dowel rods 1-inch to 1¹/₄-inch diameter and fit them through holes in the sides. Alternatively, you can turn handles (FIG. 3-5D) with 1-inch dowel ends and a max-

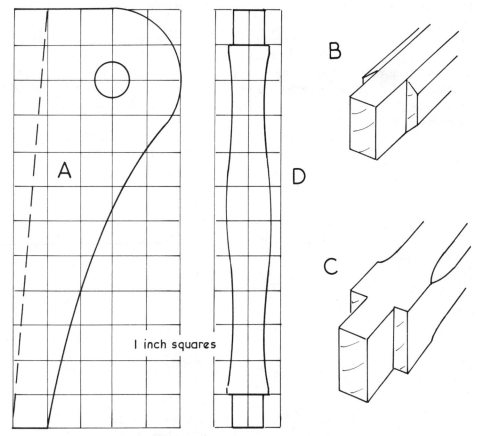

Fig. 3-5. Shapes of parts of the box with end handles.

imum diameter of 1¹/₄ inch, which is the largest grip that most people would regard as comfortable.

4. Prepare the parts for joining. It is possible to use dowels, but that is not the traditional method. You also could use nails or screws.

5. An original dough box would not have been treated, but you can finish the wood to suit your purpose. An attractive hardwood can be varnished. Paint is more suitable for outdoor use. For regular outdoor use, put strips under the ends to act as feet and to keep the bottom off the ground.

Pioneer Chest

Some settler's chests were quite large, since they had to hold most of the family possessions. Some were quite crude, but others were strong well-made pieces of furniture. A smaller version of one of these better chests can be used as a blanket box, tool chest, toy box or container for many household goods. This chest (FIG.

3-6) is a moderate size (FIG. 3-7A), but you can make a chest of any other size in the same way.

The chest can be made of softwood and the main parts are $^5/_8$ inch thick when finished. For a traditional chest all the parts should be made from solid wood, but the bottom can be made of plywood without detracting from the appearance. If boards must be joined to make up the width, stagger the joints between the sides and ends so they do not come opposite each other. The sizes may have to vary to suit available wood.

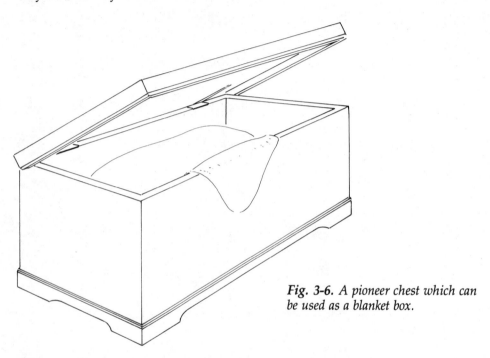

Fig. 3-6. *A pioneer chest which can be used as a blanket box.*

Materials List
for Pioneer Chest

2 sides	$^5/_8$	×	12	×	26
2 ends	$^5/_8$	×	12	×	14
1 bottom	$^5/_8$	×	$10^3/_4$	×	25
2 bottom frames	$^5/_8$	×	$1^1/_2$	×	25
2 bottom frames	$^5/_8$	×	$1^1/_2$	×	13
2 plinths	$^1/_2$	×	$2^1/_2$	×	28
2 plinths	$^1/_2$	×	$2^1/_2$	×	16
1 lid	$^5/_8$	×	$12^1/_4$	×	27
2 lid frames	$^5/_8$	×	$1^1/_2$	×	27
2 lid frames	$^5/_8$	×	$1^1/_2$	×	15
1 lid edge	$^1/_2$	×	$2^1/_4$	×	27
2 lid edges	$^1/_2$	×	$2^1/_4$	×	15

1. Prepare wood for the back, front and ends.
2. There are several possible ways of joining the corners. The best chests had through dovetails (FIG. 3-8A). These corners are very strong and have a good country look which can be left exposed as examples of your workmanship. The finger joint is a modern alternative (FIG. 3-8B). This was not used on early chests, but it is strong and acceptable, particularly if it is covered by paint. Many early chests were nailed and the joints were reinforced by nailing on thin metal straps (FIG. 3-8C). This arrangement gives a traditional look. You can make a stronger nailed joint by notching one piece over the other to take nails both ways (FIG. 3-8D).
3. Mark out and cut the corner joints of your choice and join the four boards squarely. Remove the excess glue and level any outside projections.
4. Fit the bottom inside over the frame of strips (FIG. 3-7B and C). Cut the bottom and the frame so it fits closely inside the box. Nail and glue the bottom to the frame and through the sides of the box. Nail heads will be hidden by the plinth outside. If you use a plywood bottom, it doesn't have to be more than a 1/2 inch thick. A solid wood bottom might be made with the grain lengthwise, but many early chests were made with bottoms formed with boards of random width, laid crosswise and not always glued together.
5. The plinth (FIG. 3-7D) goes all around the box and projects 1 inch below the bottom edge. This kept early boxes clear of a dirt floor, but it is still a worthwhile way to arrange the bottom of the chest. Cut the strips too long at first. Then mark and cut the shaped ends (FIG. 3-8E) to form the feet.
6. The simplest treatment for the top edges is a chamfer, but you can mold them (FIG. 3-8F).
7. It is possible to miter the corners of the plinth, but a miter cannot be very strong and the wood may split if the chest is pulled about or knocked. It is simpler and more traditional to cut the end pieces level with the sides and overlap the back and front pieces (FIG. 3-7E). Glue and nail the plinth to the chest sides and ends. Nail the overlaps.
8. Cut the board for the lid (FIG. 3-7F) so it is level at the back (FIG. 3-7G) and has about 1/8 inch clearance at the ends and front (FIG. 3-7H).
9. Frame it in the same way to the bottom (FIG. 3-7J).
10. Edge the front and ends of the top. Leave the rear edge uncovered, so it can swing up and back on its hinges.
11. Chamfer or mold the lower edges of the lid edge pieces so the edges of the plinth match. Although the lid edges may not be as vulnerable as the corners of the plinth and can be mitered at the corners, it is better to overlap them (FIG. 3-7K).
12. You can use two stout 3-inch or 4-inch butt hinges, but it is better to use T hinges (FIG. 3-8G) about 7 inches long. Arrange them 5 inches from the corners. Notch the box edge. Put strips that are as thick as the frame under the long pieces of the hinges. When each hinge is in its notch the

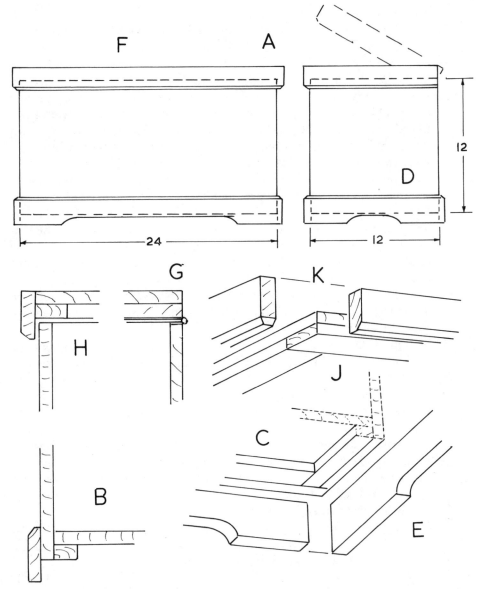

Fig. 3-7. Sizes and details of the pioneer chest.

lid should shut closely on the chest edges without being so tight that it strains the hinges.

13. Softwood is best finished with paint, although you can use a clear finish if you want the grain and joint details exposed. The outside should be given a dark finish, but a lighter color can be used inside.

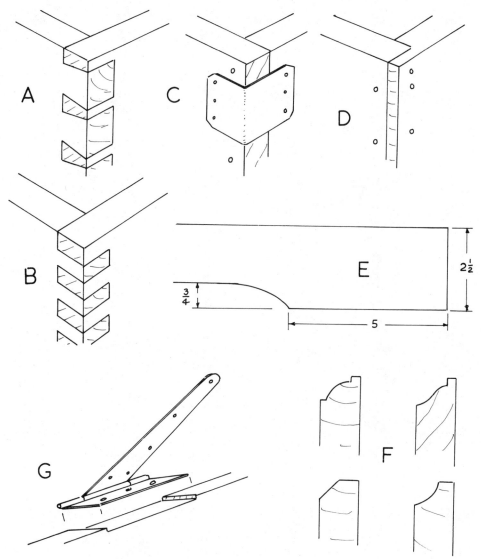

Fig. 3-8. Joints and details of the pioneer chest.

Dado Box with Tray

Making a lid to fit a box exactly is often difficult. One way to get a perfect fit is making the box and its lid as one unit and then separating them. This can be done with boxes of many constructions, but the following example shows a box containing a tray with dado joints at the corners (FIG. 3-9). It can be made as large as a chest, or quite small for jewelry. This one is drawn as a container to use on a table or for storing things under it (FIG. 3-10A).

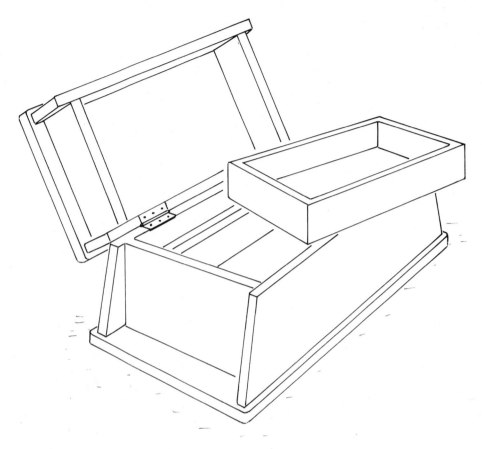

Fig. 3-9. This box has dado joints and a lift-out tray.

**Materials List
for Dado Box with Tray**

2 sides	$1/2$	×	8	×	20
2 ends	$1/2$	×	8	×	11
1 bottom	$1/2$	×	$91/2$	×	20
1 top	$1/2$	×	$91/2$	×	18
2 runners	$1/2$	×	$1/2$	×	16
2 tray sides	$3/8$	×	2	×	16
2 tray ends	$3/8$	×	2	×	11
1 tray bottom	$1/4$	×	8	×	16

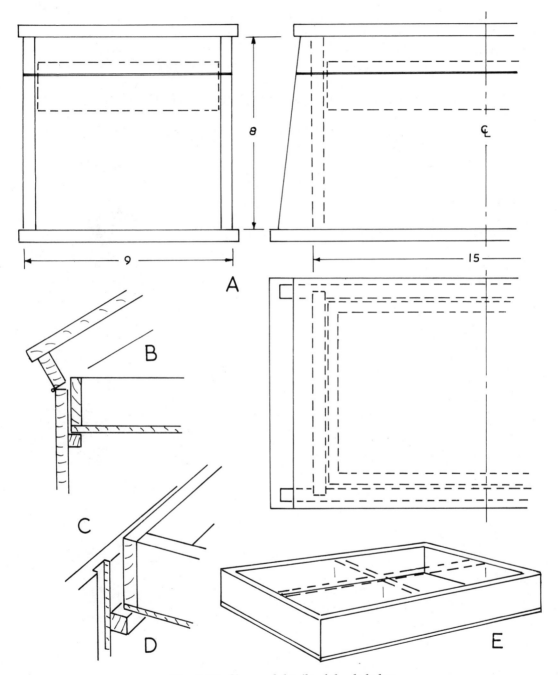

Fig. 3-10. Sizes and details of the dado box.

A compact hardwood, given a clear finish, is the best material to use. If you use softwood, it might be painted, which would be similar to many boxes produced in earlier days. The sections of wood suggested are for a light box made of hardwood. The thicknesses should be increased a little for softwood.

1. Mark the two sides (FIG. 3-11A), including the line that will cut the lid from the box.
2. Cut the two ends to size with the grain across. Mark on the cut line to match those on the sides.
3. Cut dado grooves across the sides (FIG. 3-11B and C). Make these tight fits on the ends. Cut the sloping ends of the sides.
4. Join the sides and ends. An original box had nails with ornamental heads driven in the ends through the dados. You can use ordinarly nails with heads exposed, or punch them below the surface and cover with plugs.

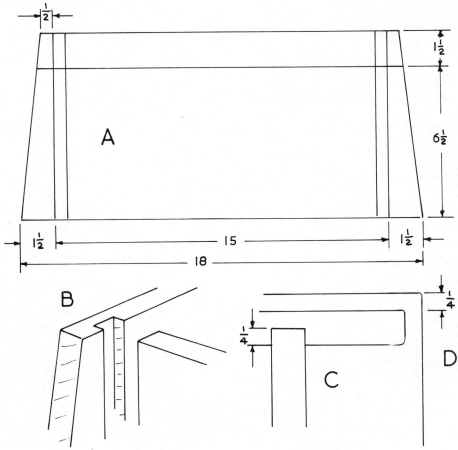

Fig. 3-11. Setting out the joints in the dado box.

5. Make the bottom 1/4 inch larger than the assembled parts (FIG. 3-11D).
6. Make the top in the same way.
7. Lightly round the corners and edges of the top and bottom and the sloping ends of the sides.
8. Join the top and bottom to the other parts. Glue may be sufficient, but you can use a few pins as well, mainly to prevent movement during gluing.
9. When the glue is set, cut around the line making the depth of the lid. You can do this by hand or against the fence of a table saw. Mark the matching sides of the lid and box so they aren't turned around by mistake during assembly.
10. Plane both sawn edges level.
11. The tray fits inside on runners and stands 1/2 inch above the top of the box (FIG. 3-10B and C). The tray may be 2 inches deep.
12. Fit two runners inside to support the tray (FIG. 3-10D).
13. Make sure the tray fits easily inside the box. Use any of the usual corner joints, and glue and pin the bottom on.
14. The tray can be left as an open box, or divisions can be included to suit the intended use (FIG. 3-10E).
15. Round the top edges of the tray. It should fit easily, but if one way fits better than the other, mark the hinged side.
16. Use two, 2-inch hinges. Fasten them to the lid and box edges so the lid closes fairly closely. The higher edges of the tray will act as dust stops.
17. Finish to suit the wood and surroundings. A clear finish inside will help show the contents.

Stacking Bins

Many things are best stored in boxes with access from the top and front. Vegetables in quantity are examples. A gardener will wish to store small tools, seeds and his other needs. In a shop you may wish to store nuts and bolts, pieces of wood or metal and innumerable other items that would otherwise get lost or make the place untidy.

Stackable bins allow you to vary your storage arrangements and move one bin without affecting the others. These stacking bins (FIG. 3-12) are not too big to be lifted individually when filled with a moderate load. They are shown with a single division, but you can leave that out or make other internal divisions. The sizes suggested (FIG. 3-13A) occupy a floor space 12 inches by 24 inches, and three bins are about 32 inches high. You might make any number of bins and stack them higher or arrange the stacks beside each other. You might make one bin and follow with others later, but it is easier to get sizes matching exactly if all the bins you want are made at the same time. The instructions are for one bin, but if you make several them you should make all the matching parts for all the bins before moving to the next stage.

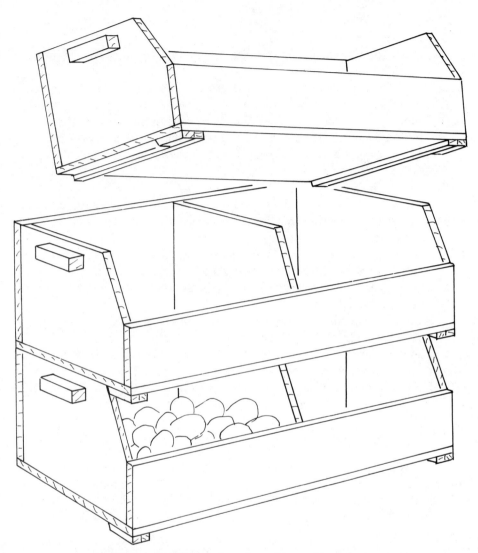

Fig. 3-12. This design allows bins to be stacked.

**Materials List
for Stacking Bins (one bin)**

2 ends	5/8	× 10	× 14
1 division	5/8	× 10	× 14
1 back	5/8	× 10	× 26
1 front	5/8	× 5	× 26
1 bottom	5/8	× 13 1/4 ×	26
feet from	5/8	× 5/8 ×	32

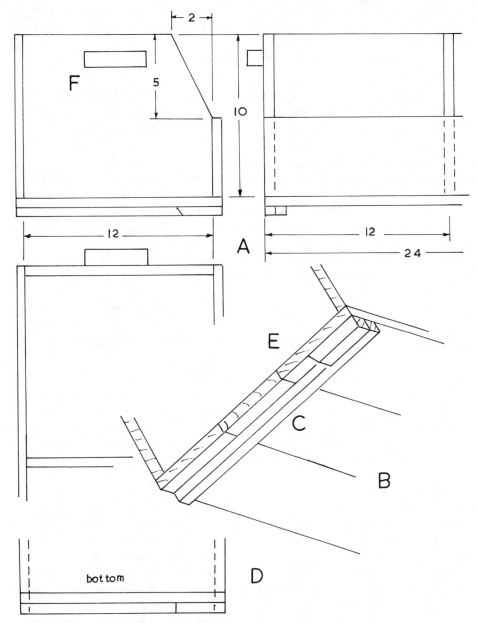

Fig. 3-13. Sizes and construction of a stacking bin.

All wood is ⁵/8-inch finished thickness, but using other available wood should make little difference. Nail or screw all the parts. Use glue as well if you wish. Arrange the nails closer together near the openings. Softwood is satisfactory for most purposes. Bins used indoors, or which may get hard usage, might be made of hardwood, but this adds to the weight.

1. Both ends and the division are the same. Make them with the grain from front to back. The slope can be hollowed, instead of straight, if you prefer the appearance.
2. Make the back and front to match the heights of the ends. Mark on the position of the division.
3. Nail the parts together. Check levels across the top and bottom.
4. The bottom can be made from several boards (FIG. 3-13B) to make up the width. For most purposes, glue is not needed for the edges. The bottom can be a little oversized so the edges can be trimmed level after assembly.
5. The bins must be assembled squarely so they can fit together properly in any order. Check the squareness as you nail the bottom. Trim edges level and square.
6. Guides are needed under the ends of the bin to act as feet and to ensure a bin fits securely on the one below (FIG. 3-13C). Allow a 1/8-inch clearance for ease in stacking, but do not make too loose a fit.
7. Put a strip across the full width of the bottom at each end to fit inside the top of the bin below (FIG. 3-13D). Put another piece outside this (FIG. 3-13E) cut to fit against the slope of the next bin front.
8. The handles are 4-inch lengths of 1 inch square strip (FIG. 3-13F), securely nailed or screwed from inside. For most purposes, you don't need to shape or round them excessively. Take the sharpness off the exposed edges and corners.
9. Round the edges where your hand might make contact in dealing with the contents of bins. Besides the slopes of the ends and the division and the front piece, round the front part of the bottom of each bin where it comes above the one below.
10. For many purposes you may leave the wood untreated. If you paint the wood, a light color inside helps to show up the contents.

Desk

A tabletop desk was an essential piece of furniture in early homes. It held family documents, papers, writing materials and letters. It provided a writing surface at a convenient angle. Nowadays, we accept a flat writing surface, but if you want to draw or lay out charts a sloping top is more convenient. Such a desk also takes care of the same sort of things it did in the earlier days, particularly in a home where the amount of paperwork does not justify anything more elaborate.

This desk (FIG. 3-14A) is intended to be used on a table. It is not too heavy or large to be moved about (FIG. 3-15A) and can be fitted with legs (FIG. 3-14B) for use by a child. When the child grows out of it, the legs can be removed and the desk moved to a table top.

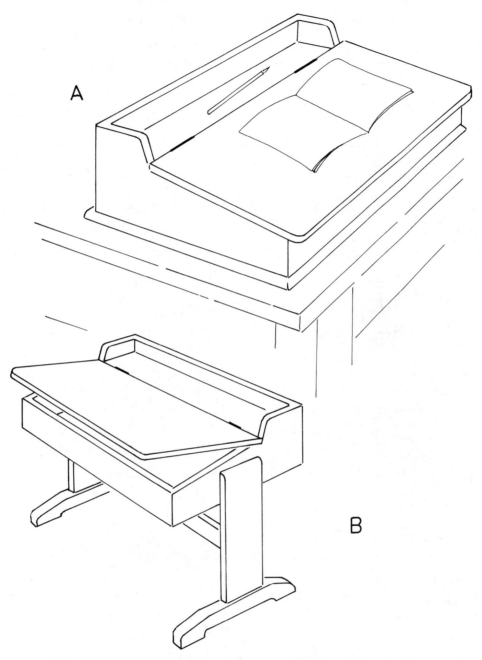

Fig. 3-14. This desk can be used on a table or fitted with its own legs.

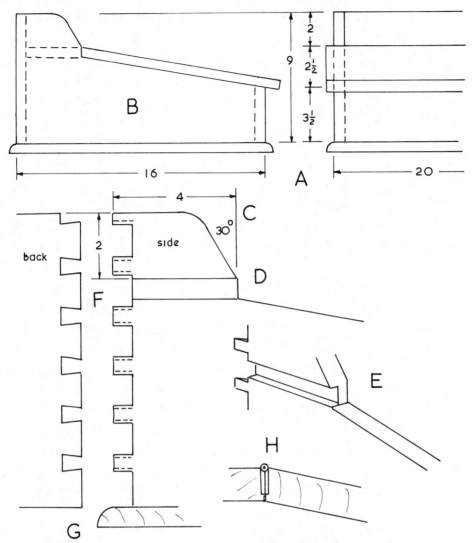

Fig. 3-15. Sizes and joints of the desk.

Materials List for Desk

2 sides	$5/8$	×	9	×	18
1 back	$5/8$	×	9	×	22
1 front	$5/8$	×	4	×	22
1 top	$5/8$	×	$3^1/2$	×	21
1 flap	$5/8$	×	13	×	23
1 bottom	$5/8$	×	16	×	23
2 legs	$3/4$	×	6	×	19
2 feet	$1^1/4$	×	3	×	16
1 rail	1	×	3	×	24

Hardwood between 1/2 inch and 5/8 inch finished thickness can be used for most parts of the desk. With a stained and clear finish, the desk is suitable for any room. If a child is the sole user you might use softwood and paint it. In that case, do not use wood thinner than 5/8 inch. Construction is described with dovetailed corners, which were used in a good quality early desk. You can use any of the other corner joints or just nail or screw the corners. The bottom is screwed or nailed from below.

1. Mark out the pair of sides (FIGS. 3-15B and 16A). Cut the top edges to the level of the flat top and slope to 30° (FIG. 3-15C). The sloping edges act as stops when the flap is raised.
2. Cut the wood for the back (FIG. 3-16B). At the corners, mark the thicknesses of the other parts on all ends.
3. Cut the dado grooves to suit the wood that will be used for the top (FIG. 3-15D and E). The underside must be level with the sloping side so the flap will fit properly.
4. Dovetails at the rear corners must be arranged so the grooves are opposite the sockets (FIG. 3-15F), where they will be hidden by tails. Arrange this to suit your dovetailing equipment, but if you are cutting by hand, a suitable arrangement is shown.

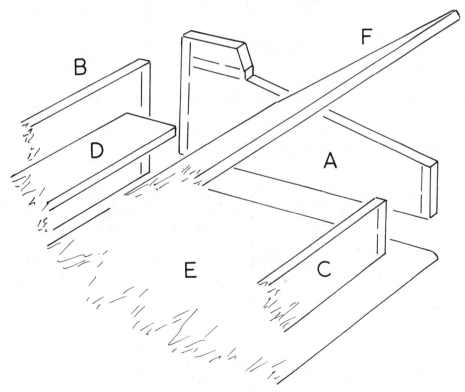

Fig. 3-16. How the desk parts fit together.

5. Cut the front (FIG. 3-16C) the same length as the back. Bevel its top edge to match the slope of the sides. Cut dovetail joints similar to those at the rear, but make sure there are no spacing problems.

6. The top (FIG. 3-16D) should fit closely against the back and its front edge should be level with the cutdown parts of the sides. This front edge must not come behind these edges and it is better if it is 1/16 inch in front, so the flap will swing without restriction.

7. Join these parts. Clamp the dovetails tightly. Check squareness by comparing diagonal measurements. Level the dovetails after the glue sets. Remove any surplus glue inside.

8. Make the bottom (FIG. 3-16E) to project 1/2 inch all around. You will probably have to glue boards to make up the width. You can either square the edges or make them rounded (FIG. 3-15G). Glue and screw the bottom on from below. Countersink the screw heads below the surface so there is no risk of scratching a tabletop.

9. Make the flap (FIG. 3-16F) so it projects 1/2 inch at the sides and 3/4 inch at the front. Bevel the upper edge to fit against the top. You will probably have to glue boards to make up the width. If you have doubts about the flap remaining flat, you can screw 5/8-inch by 11/2-inch battens across the bottom to fit easily inside the desk when the flap is closed. Use screws without glue to allow a little expansion and contraction without risking cracking or warping.

10. Use two 2-inch brass hinges between the flap and the top. Drill them so the joint is tight when closed. Arrange the hinge knuckles so the centers of the pins are in line with the meeting surfaces (FIG. 3-15H). This allows the flap to lift sufficiently without the hinges making too much of a projection above the working surfaces.

11. That completes the construction of a tabletop desk. Round the exposed edges and corners, particularly the front of the flap. Finish to suit the wood. You might glue cloth on the underside to reduce slipping or marking a polished tabletop.

12. If you want to make a child's desk that can be used when sitting on a stool or low chair, you can add a pair of legs with a footbar (FIG. 3-17). Test the height with your child on the seat that will be used, and arrange the leg lengths accordingly.

13. The two feet are thicker (FIG. 3-17A) to help stability. Mark them, but do not cut the bottom or slopes until the joints are prepared.

14. Mark out the legs (FIG. 3-17B) with the joint details and the position of the footbar.

15. The traditional way of joining the legs to the feet is with mortise and tenon joints (FIG. 3-17C). You can use 3/8-inch dowels (FIG. 3-17D). Cut the feet to shape after cutting mortises or drilling for dowels.

16. The footbar can be tenoned (FIG. 3-17E), or you can dowel to the legs. Cut the footbar so it will space the legs to match the width of the desk.

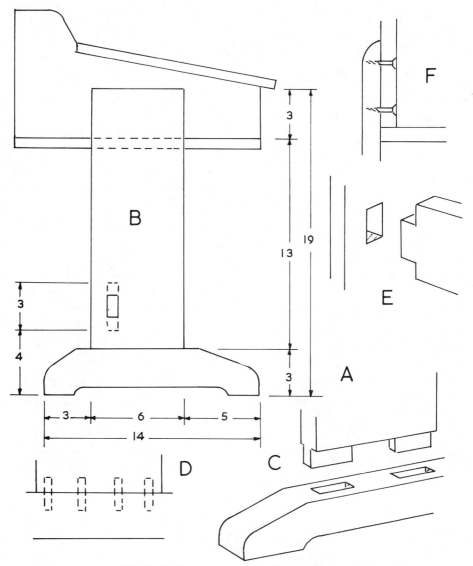

Fig. 3-17. Leg arrangements for the desk.

17. Either level the edges of the whole desk bottom to allow the legs to fit against the sides, or notch the projecting edge to fit them. Arrange the legs to fit centrally on the sides.

18. Round the tops of the legs. If you arrange them to come high on the sides, it is possible to raise the desk later by about 2 inches to suit a growing child.

19. Glue the legs to the feet and the footbar to the sides, but use screws without glue to hold the desk to the legs (FIG. 3-17F). Check that desk bottom and feet are parallel.

4

Hanging furniture

Early homes had many things hung on the wall. This kept them clean and away from what might have only been a dirt floor. It is still convenient in most homes to arrange some furniture on the walls. Some of the early furniture may not be needed for its original purpose, but it is attractive when applied to other uses. Shelves always provide places to store books and a great many small items for utility or display. A wall cupboard has an ongoing use. We might not want to provide hanging boxes for salt or clay pipes, but reproductions of these containers can store packet foods in a kitchen, a flower pot on an inside or outside wall, kitchen tools, or office needs.

Hanging furniture makes use of space that might otherwise remain bare. It also serves a decorative and useful purpose without using up valuable floor space. A hanging piece may go above another item of furniture standing on the floor, so two pieces of furniture can go over one area of floor. Most pieces of hanging furniture are comparatively small and simple, so they are easy to make in one weekend.

Hanging Boxes

Boxes attached to the wall once contained many of the pioneer family possessions. Many were hasty and basic constructions, but as homes became more comfortable and other furniture was used for storage, the number of hanging boxes was reduced and the remainder became more decorative. If you are furnishing a room in a fairly primitive fashion, or you want simple boxes on the wall for gardening or other outside purposes, you can make plain boxes. If you want to maintain an Early American appearance while conforming to a later or more modern period, very similar hanging boxes can be made of better wood, with a more ornate design and a painted or polished finish.

Early boxes were made from local woods. For authentic reproductions you should use wood from your own region. There is no place for plywood. Both hardwoods and softwoods are appropriate.

A simple hanging box (FIG. 4-1A) can be made to any size. A small one might hold pegs, darts, or other small items. A larger box might support a potted plant. The suggested sizes (FIG. 4-2A) can vary to suit your needs. The back, front, and bottom should come between the sides (FIG. 4-2B). The weight is then across the

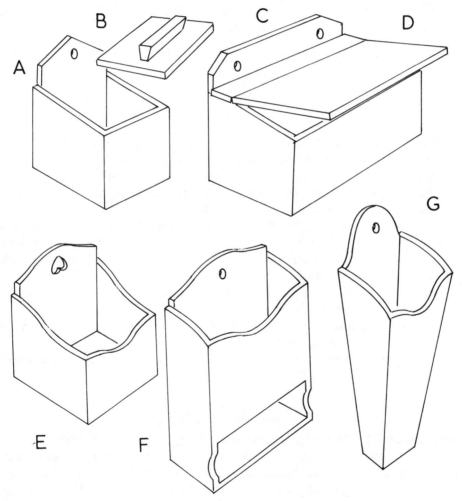

Fig. 4-1. Boxes of many types can be made to hang on a wall.

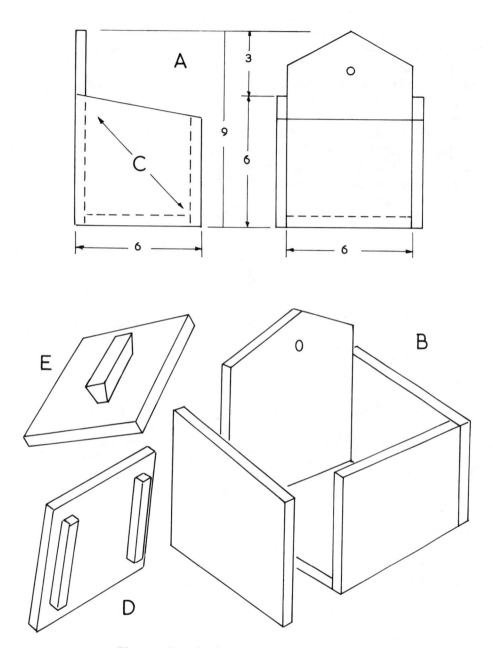

Fig. 4-2. Details of a simple hanging box with lid.

nails, instead of in a direction that would tend to pull them out. If the load is heavy, you need to provide greater support by arranging the grain of the side pieces diagonally (FIG. 4-2C). Use cut nails for a primitive reproduction, otherwise set round nails below the surface and cover their heads with stopping.

You can make a lift-off lid (FIG. 4-1B) by attaching strips inside (FIG. 4-2D) and a wood handle on top (FIG. 4-2E).

The simple box is intended to hang on a nail or peg and may swing. Providing a pair of hanging holes may be better (FIG. 4-1C). In both cases, holes should be large enough to lift the box off the nails or pegs, unless you require it permanently in place.

A hinged lid can be attached to a simple box, but it is better to arrange a narrow flat part (FIG. 4-1D), then the lid and its strip overhang slightly (FIG. 4-3A). As with the first box, sizes can vary to suit your needs. Two plain or decorative hinges can be screwed on the surface (FIG. 4-3B). In an original box they were not let into the thickness.

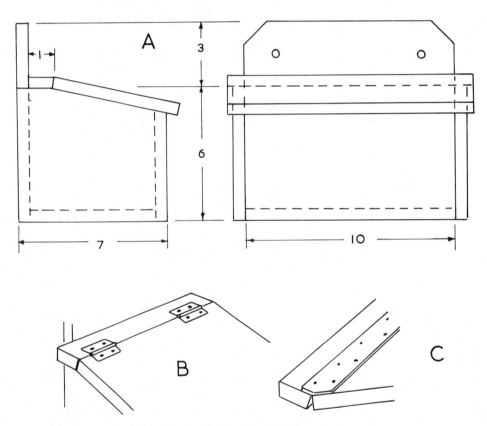

Fig. 4-3. Sizes and methods of hinging a hanging box.

Putting the hinges on top leaves a narrow gap where moisture might seep. If the box will hang outdoors, it is better to use the pioneer's method of covering the meeting edges with a strip of leather nailed right across as a hinge (FIG. 4-3C).

A more ornate hanging box can be made in a generally similar way, with all the upper edges curved (FIG. 4-1E). The top of the back can be arranged so it hangs on one or two nails (FIG. 4-4A and B). You can use round hanging holes, but inverted hearts tie in well with the curved outlines (FIG. 4-4C).

A more upright box with a shelf is another possibility (FIG. 4-1F). In the sizes

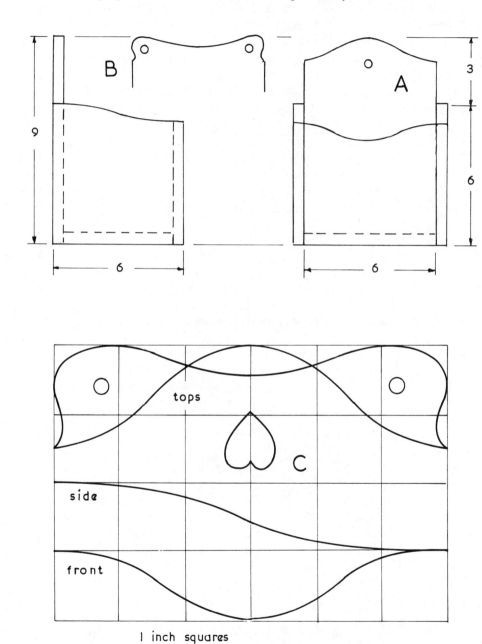

Fig. 4-4. *Decorative shaping for a hanging box.*

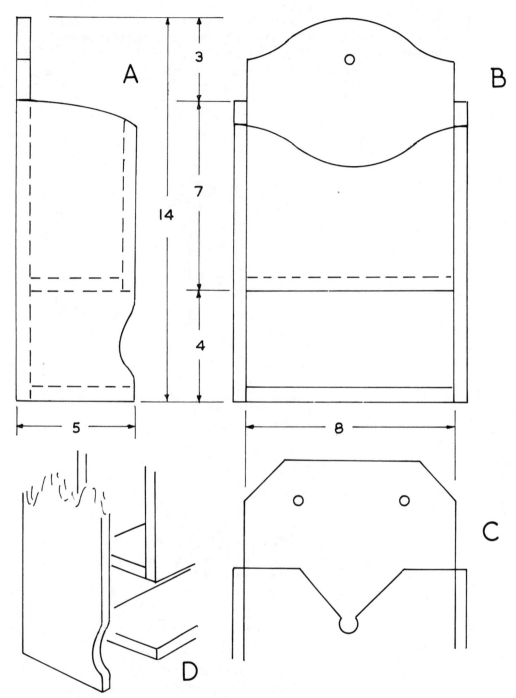

Fig. 4-5. *This hanging box also has a shelf.*

suggested, this is suitable for shoe cleaning materials (FIG. 4-5A). You can use curves and one or two hanging holes (FIG. 4-5B), similar to the previous box, or have straight lines, with a V cut into a hole to provide front access (FIG. 4-5C). Fit the front between the sides and bring the bottom to the same level (FIG. 4-5D).

Hanging boxes for clay "churchwarden" pipes were tall and narrow and might be tapered both ways (FIG. 4-1G). It can be used just as a decoration, or for a place to store anything in tall rod form. A wide taper affects the angles you plane, but a slight taper (FIG. 4-6A) does not need any special treatment. During assembly you can plane edges square and trim them, if necessary.

The dipped front (FIG. 4-6B) gives easy access, but the front top edge can be made straight across, if that better holds your intended contents.

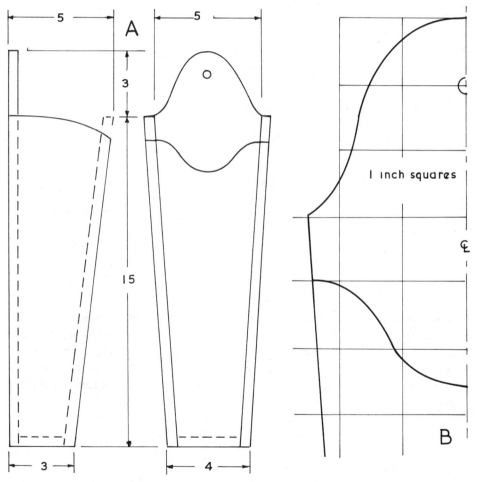

Fig. 4-6. A tall box was used for clay pipes, but has may modern uses.

FIGURE 4-2

1 back	1/2 × 6	× 10
2 sides	1/2 × 6	× 7
1 front	1/2 × 5	× 7
1 bottom	1/2 × 5	× 7

FIGURE 4-3

1 back	1/2 × 9	× 11
2 sides	1/2 × 6	× 8
1 front	1/2 × 5	× 11
1 bottom	1/2 × 6	× 11
1 lid strip	1/2 × 1	× 13
1 lid	1/2 × 7	× 13

FIGURE 4-4

1 back	1/2 × 6	× 10
2 sides	1/2 × 6	× 7
1 front	1/2 × 5	× 7
1 bottom	1/2 × 5	× 7

FIGURE 4-5

1 back	1/2 × 8	× 15
2 sides	1/2 × 5	× 13
1 front	1/2 × 7	× 9
1 shelf	1/2 × 4	× 9
1 bottom	1/2 × 4 1/2 ×	9

FIGURE 4-6

1 back	1/2 × 5	× 19
2 sides	1/2 × 5	× 16
1 front	1/2 × 5	× 15
1 bottom	1/2 × 2	× 4

Block of Shelves

Shelves arranged between a pair of uprights are used as much now as they were in early days. Although the basic idea is simple, many variations are possible, particularly in the way the ends and shelves are decorated. However, the purpose is usually utilitarian, and the contents of the shelves may be more decorative than the surrounding woodwork. Shelves that are primarily functional make a good traditional furniture project.

Any of the many ways of attaching shelves to the ends were used, so you can choose what seems appropriate. If the shelves will be used in a garage or less-important place, you need not use such advanced joints as may be required for living room furniture.

Nailing through the ends is the simplest way of attaching shelves (FIG. 4-7A). The drawback with this depends only on the crosswise loads on the nails for strength. This can lead to the shelf splitting.

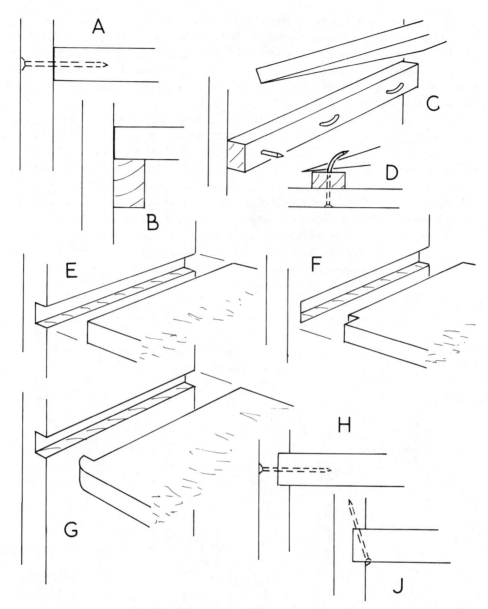

Fig. 4-7. *Joints for shelves can take many forms.*

A better way is to support the shelf on a cleat (FIG. 4-7B). In modern construction we screw the cleat in place, but screws were not used in early assemblies. An alternative is to take nails through and clench them (FIG. 4-7C). Turn each nail first over a spike to curve it (FIG. 4-7D), then bury the point while supporting the head with an iron block. This makes a very strong joint, particularly suitable for outdoor work.

The standard shelf-to-end joint is called a dado, although early craftsmen called it by the English name of housing joint. The standard form has the groove cut right through (FIG. 4-7E). For a neater appearance at the front, you can use a stopped dado (FIG. 4-7F). Another way of hiding the groove is by making the shelf wider so it overlaps the groove (FIG. 4-7G). The groove may also be hidden by a lip, as used in this project.

Glue does not hold well on end grain, and a shelf in a groove has end grain exposed to glue in all directions. If other parts of the assembly help resist these joints pulling open, glue alone may be sufficient. Otherwise each joint can be nailed (FIG. 4-7H). If you do not want nail heads showing outside, nail diagonally from below (FIG. 4-7J). Fine screws can be used, but not if you want to make an authentic reproduction. In a block of several shelves, you can add sufficient strength by nailing or screwing upwards at two positions at the ends of the top and bottom shelves, and gluing the other joints.

The block of shelves in FIG. 4-8 can be used as a bookcase or display rack for plates and souvenirs. It serves as a place to put many things to keep them from

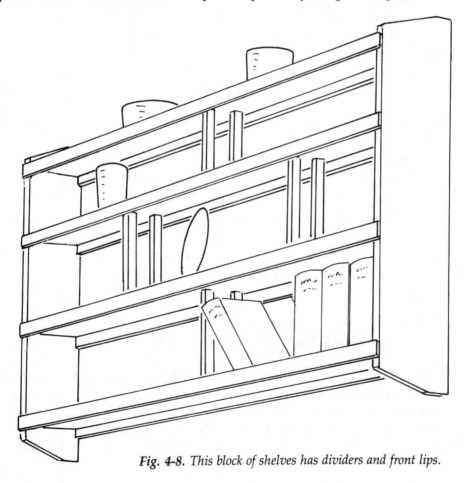

Fig. 4-8. This block of shelves has dividers and front lips.

cluttering tables and other furniture. If made from hardwood and given a good finish, the shelves can go in a living room. Made from softwood and given a painted finish, they can be used in a garage or workshop.

As drawn (FIG. 4-9), the unit projects 8 inches from the wall and is just over 3 feet square. Lips on the shelf edges prevent small items from rolling off and act as stops if display items are tilted. The back is open to the wall surface, except for

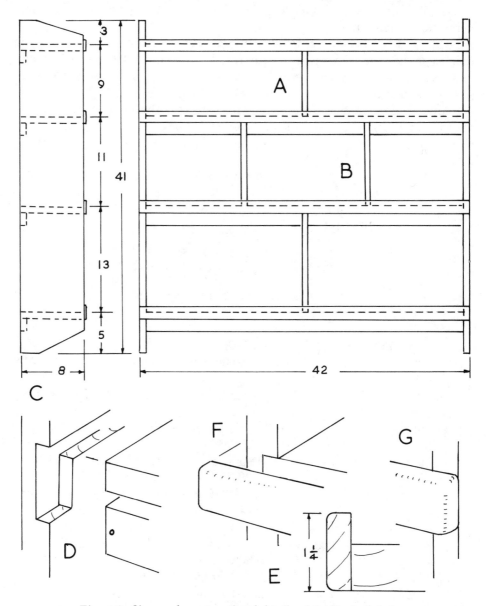

Fig. 4-9. Sizes and constructional details of the block of shelves.

pieces under the rear edges of the shelves. They provide rigidity, and can be used for screws through to the wall. Depths between shelves are graduated. If you alter sizes, remember that any unit of this type looks best with spaces becoming progressively smaller towards the top.

Dividers are suggested (FIG. 4-9A and B). These serve two purposes. First, they provide mutual help—if one shelf is heavily loaded, the next shelf helps hold it and prevents sagging. Second, if a space is only partially filled with books, dividers prevent the books from falling over and allow you to separate items on the same shelf.

The dividers can be rectangular or turned. Turned spindles were used more than might have been expected in early furniture. A simple lathe is not difficult to make and a presentable turned piece was easier to make than a straight squared section from hewn wood, using hand tools.

Any of the suggested ways of joining the shelves to the ends can be used, but the following instructions assume dado joints will be cut.

Materials List for
Block of Shelves

2 sides	$3/4 \times 8 \times 43$
4 shelves	$3/4 \times 8 \times 45$
4 stiffeners	$3/4 \times 1^{1}/2 \times 45$
4 lips	$3/8 \times 1^{1}/4 \times 45$
2 dividers	$3/4 \times 1$ or $1^{1}/4 \times 1^{1}/4 \times 14$
4 dividers	$3/4 \times 1$ or $1^{1}/4 \times 1^{1}/4 \times 12$
2 dividers	$3/4 \times 1$ or $1^{1}/4 \times 1^{1}/4 \times 10$

1. Mark out the pair of sides (FIG. 4-9C).
2. Cut the grooves slightly less than halfway through the wood and tightly fit on the shelf material.
3. Make notches at the back to the same depth for the stiffening pieces (FIG. 4-9D).
4. Cut the ends of the sides to shape. Curves can be used instead of straight cuts, if you wish.
5. Cut the shelves and their stiffening pieces all to the same length, with squared ends.
6. Mark the shelves for the dividers (FIG. 4-10A). The arrangement shown can vary to suit your needs, or you can omit dividers in one space.
7. If you use rectangular dividers, make their lengths between shoulders equal to the spacings between the dado grooves on the ends, and allow for tenons (FIG. 4-10B) into the shelves.
8. If you prefer turned spindles, get their lengths in the same way and turn the dowel ends to fit into holes in the shelves. Spindles can be turned to

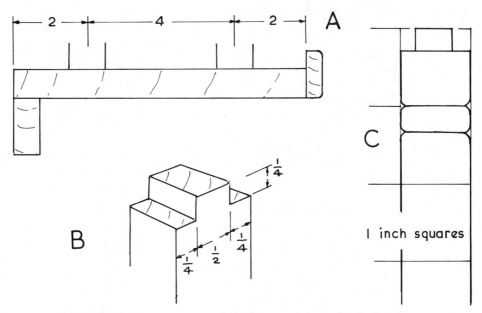

Fig. 4-10. The arrangement of dividing posts in the block of shelves.

any design desired, but a simple arrangement at each end is suggested (FIG. 4-10C), making the greater part of the length a simple cylinder.

9. Cut mortises or drill holes for the divider ends in the shelves.
10. Assemble the shelves to the ends. Work on a flat surface to prevent twist and check squareness by comparing diagonal measurements.
11. Prepare wood for the lips, with the fronts rounded (FIG. 4-9E).
12. Cut the lips to reach the outsides of the sides and round the outer edges and corners (FIG. 4-9F and G).
13. Fit the lips in place with glue and a few fine nails set below the surface and covered with stopping.
14. Drill the stiffening strips for screws to the wall. Most of the load can be taken by two or three screws under the top shelf, but more may be required in other strips.
15. Finish with paint or stain and polish.

Hanging Cabinet

After making a block of shelves, the next step is to make a cabinet with a door to protect and hide the contents. Such hanging cabinets are used today as much as in earlier days. This cabinet (FIG. 4-11) is made of solid wood throughout and has a capacity about 8 inches square 12 inches high. The size can vary depending on the widths of the boards used.

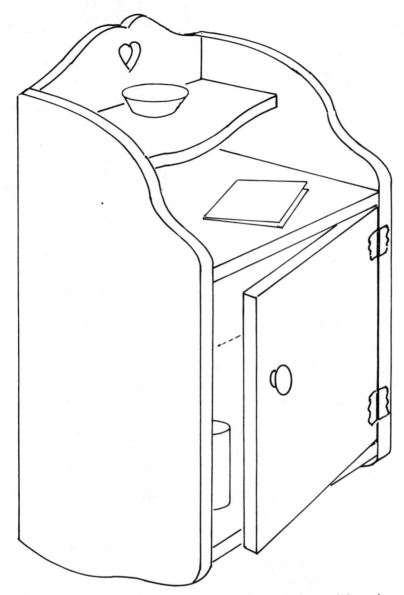

Fig. 4-11. This hanging cabinet with shelf is made from solid wood.

For a cabinet of the suggested size (FIG. 4-12), use boards 8 inches wide for the main parts. They should be hardwood for a good-quality finish, but softwood can be used and painted. For a traditional appearance, wood 5/8 inch thick should be used, but you can reduce this a little, if you wish. Some parts can be joined with dowels, which are not traditional, but since they won't show, they will not affect the appearance.

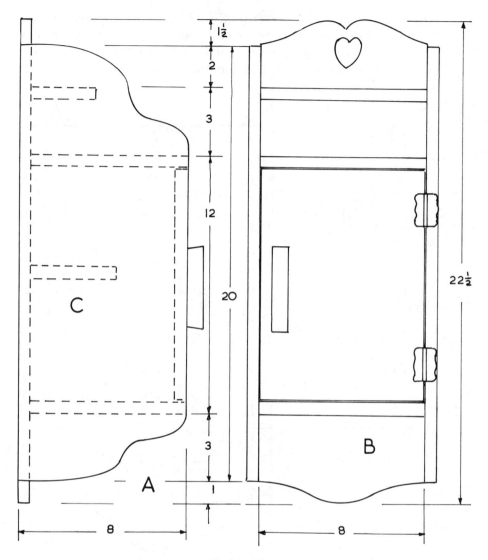

Fig. 4-12. Sizes of the small cabinet.

**Materials List
for Hanging Cabinet**

2 sides	$5/8$	× 8		× 22
1 back	$5/8$	× 8		× 25
1 top	$5/8$	× $7^3/8$	× 10
1 bottom	$5/8$	× $7^3/8$	× 10
2 shelves	$5/8$	× 4		× 10
1 door	$5/8$	× 8		× 12
1 handle	$3/4$	×	$7/8$	× 6

1. Mark out the pair of sides first (FIG. 4-12A). Allow for the back coming between the sides and mark on the positions of the top and bottom of the cabinet and the shelves. Draw the curves at the top (FIG. 4-13A) and bottom (FIG. 4-13B), but delay cutting until the dowel joints are prepared.

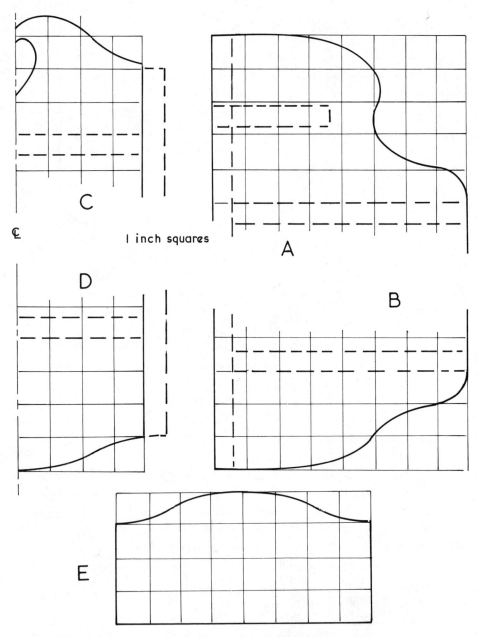

Fig. 4-13. Details of shaped parts of the small cabinet.

2. The back (FIG. 4-12B) extends above and below the sides (FIG. 4-13C and D). Mark the positions of the other parts so they match the positions on the sides. Do not shape the ends until the joints are prepared.

3. Make the top and bottom of the cabinet level with the front edges of the sides when fitted against the back. Cut these and the inside shelf (FIG. 4-12C) the same length as the width of the back.

4. Cut the top shelf (FIG. 4-13E) with a shaped front edge. Round this edge and the front edge of the inside shelf.

5. When the cabinet is in position, its rear surface will not show, so you can drill the back of all the crosswise pieces for screws. Three #8-gauge by 1½-inch screws at each place will suffice.

6. Prepare the sides and the parts that meet them for ¼-inch dowels. Placing the holes about 2 inches apart should be suitable (FIG. 4-14A).

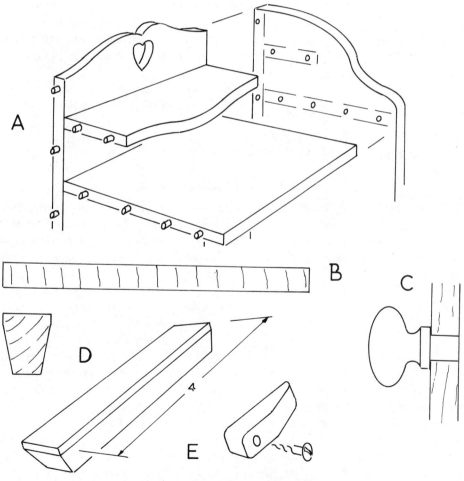

Fig. 4-14. Construction and handle details for the small cabinet.

7. When all the joints are prepared, cut the shaped ends. Sand all edges and surfaces that will be difficult to reach after assembly.

8. Glue and screw the crosswise parts to the back, then join them to the two sides with dowels. Use clamps or weights to pull the parts tightly together. The parts should hold each other squarely, but check squareness of the door opening.

9. Use a plain piece of wood for the door. If you use a piece that has been cut radially, with its end grain lines through the thickness (FIG. 4-14B) there should be no risk of it warping. Wood with other end grain patterns might warp if not fully seasoned.

10. Make the door an easy fit in the opening. You can attach the hinges to the edge, but for a traditional appearance it is better to use ornamental hinges about $1^1/2$ inches long on the surface.

11. The handle can be a turned knob glued in a hole (FIG. 4-14C), or you can make a tapered block to be held by screws from the rear of the door (FIG. 4-14D).

12. Put a small block on the cabinet side to act as a door stop. The traditional closure is a small turnbutton (FIG. 4-14E), or you can attach a ball catch into the edge of the door.

13. Two screws should be enough to hang the cabinet. The screw holes should be widely spaced inconspicuously inside, just below the top of the cabinet.

14. Finish hardwood with stain and polish or paint softwood, preferably with a lighter color inside.

Shaker-Style Coat Rack

The Shaker sect fitted rails high around the walls of a room with pegs projecting at frequent intervals. These were used to hang anything not required for immediate use, even items as large as chairs. We may not want to go that far, but rails with pegs or hooks have many uses. The Shakers had a standard type of peg and this suits a great many uses today. You can turn your own (FIG. 4-15A) or you can buy them. The pegs have dowel ends to glue into holes. For greatest security, make a saw cut across the end and drive in a glued wedge (FIG. 4-15B), then plane the end level. Arrange the wedge to expand the dowel end in the direction of the rail grain (FIG. 4-15C). Expanding the other way might split the rail.

This rack (FIG. 4-16) uses Shaker pegs for hanging coats, hats, belts, scarves, canes, and many other things around a mirror, so you can check your appearance when you dress to go out. Hardwood can be used to match other furniture, or in some places you may wish to use softwood and paint it.

Exact sizes are not important and the design can be adapted to incorporate an existing mirror. Edges can be left square or given simple bevels. Molded edges, like you can cut with a router, are appropriate. The design is shown with pegs, but you could screw on metal hooks, which are appropriate to a later period. Plastic hooks do not suit a traditional look.

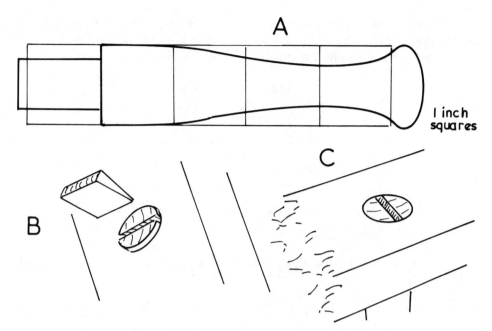

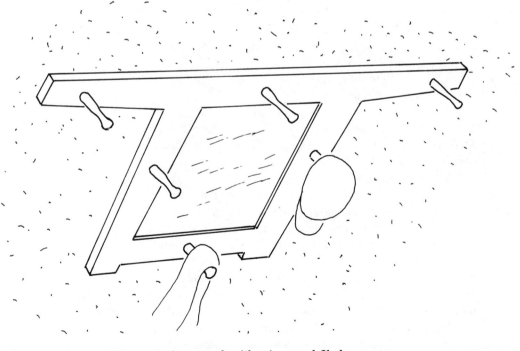

Fig. 4-15. The shape of Shaker pegs and method of securing.

Fig. 4-16. A coat rack with mirror and Shaker pegs.

The instructions and drawings allow for parts being joined with mortise and tenon joints in the traditional way. If you prefer to use dowels instead, they will be hidden, so the different construction will not be obvious.

Materials List for
Shaker-Style Coat Rack

1 top	$3/4 \times 4 \times 44$
2 sides	$3/4 \times 4 \times 24$
1 rail	$3/4 \times 3 \times 16$
4 fillets	$1/4 \times 1/4 \times 15$

1. Prepare the wood for the sides and bottom rail. The sides (FIG. 4-17A and B) will taper from 4 inches to 3 inches, but leave them 4 inches wide until after the joints are cut. The bottom rail is parallel 3 inches wide. Allow some excess length on all parts to be trimmed off when joints are marked and cut.
2. Cut rabbets for the mirror (FIG. 4-17C) on all these pieces.
3. Prepare wood for the top (FIG. 4-17D and E). Mark the positions of the sides and the tapers, but leave the wood parallel until after the joints are cut.
4. From the inner positions of the sides, mark $1/4$ inch for the rabbet, then a further 2 inches for the mortise (FIG. 4-17F) at each position. That will be the limit of the rabbet under the top (FIG. 4-17G).
5. Mark and cut the tenons on the sides (FIG. 4-18A). Each tenon is central and $1/4$ inch thick. It is 2 inches wide from the inner surface of the rabbet. Step the shoulder to fit into the top rabbet.
6. Taking the mortise and tenon 1 inch deep should be sufficient. Cut the mortises (FIG. 4-18B) to suit.
7. Check what the width between the sides will be when joined to the top. That gives you the length between shoulders of the bottom rail.
8. Mark and cut the joints in the bottom rail in a way similar to the top joints (FIG. 4-18C).
9. Cut the tapers on the top and sides.
10. Bevel the external front edges about $1/4$ inch all around. The bevels can be tapered from where the sides and top meet to their ends.
11. Six positions for pegs are shown, but this number can be altered. Mark and drill to suit the pegs. Make sure the holes are square to the surface. It is unsatisfactory for any pegs to slope downwards after fitting.
12. Assemble the parts. Check squareness. Clamp until the glue sets.
13. In an original rack the joints were strengthened with dowels through the tenons (FIG. 4-17H). With the strength of modern glues this is not essential, but you may wish to use them for the sake of appearance.
14. Try the mirror in place and prepare fillets to hold it (FIG. 4-17J), but leave final fitting until the wood is finished.

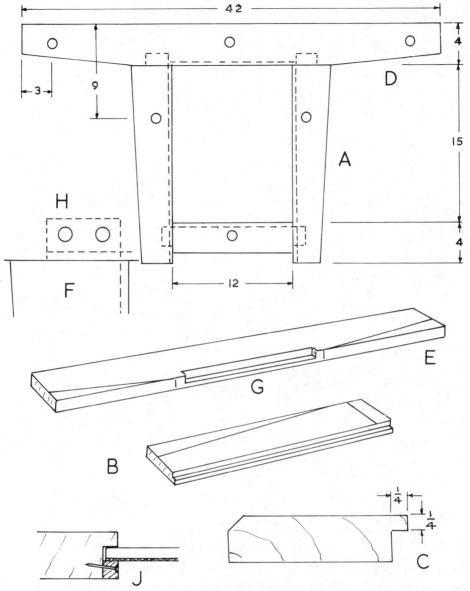

Fig. 4-17. Sizes and parts details of the Shaker-style coat rack.

15. It is advisable to stain and polish the wood before the pegs are fitted. Glue them in place and wedge them if necessary. Drill holes for screwing to the wall. A stout screw near each end may be sufficient.

16. Fit the mirror with a piece of card behind it. Fit fillets all around, with fine pins driven at an angle at widely-spaced intervals. If it is ever necessary to remove the mirror, the fillets can be prised out.

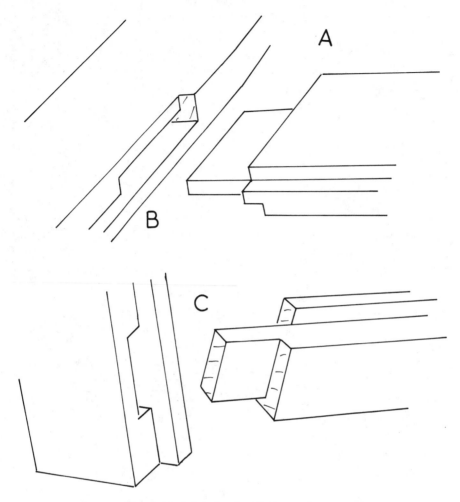

Fig. 4-18. Joints for the Shaker-style coat rack.

Wall Mirror or Picture

Early woodworkers with little skill and few tools had to exercise ingenuity to overcome limitations. Making rabbets for picture or mirror frames without a suitable tool is one such problem. The answer is putting a wider strip over a narrower one. Miters in frames are always a source of weakness, and early framemakers put squares of wood over the miters for strength and decoration. This frame for a mirror or picture (FIG. 4-19) is made that way and the design is expanded to include a shelf.

Construction is as in early frames, with the frame molding made in two thicknesses (FIG. 4-21A). The miters are covered with squares (FIG. 4-21B). Other parts are then built around to disguise the way the molding is made up. The sug-

Fig. 4-19. This frame with shelf could hold a mirror or a picture.

gested size suits a mirror or picture 12 inches by 15 inches (FIG. 4-20), but the measurements can be altered to other sizes while using the same method of construction. Frame parts are the same all around, except the bottom rear piece is widened to project below the shelf.

Any wood can be used, but for a hall or living room, the unit looks best if made from attractive hardwood and given a stained and polished finish.

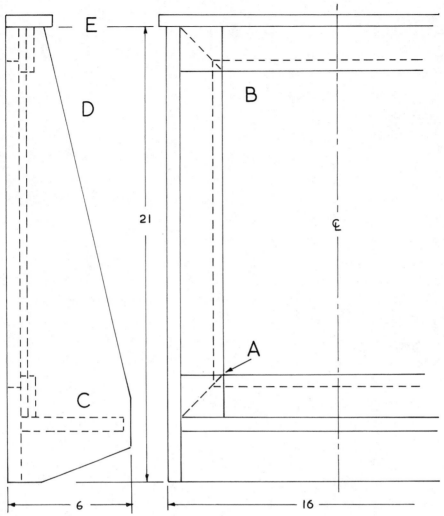

Fig. 4-20. Suggested sizes for the mirror frame.

Materials List for
Wall Mirror or Picture

2 frames	$5/8 \times 1\frac{1}{2} \times 20$
1 frame	$5/8 \times 1\frac{1}{2} \times 17$
1 frame	$5/8 \times 4\frac{1}{2} \times 17$
2 frames	$3/8 \times 2 \quad \times 20$
2 frames	$3/8 \times 2 \quad \times 17$
squares from	$3/8 \times 2 \quad \times 12$
1 shelf	$5/8 \times 5 \quad \times 17$
1 top	$1/2 \times 2\frac{1}{2} \times 18$
2 sides	$1/2 \times 6 \quad \times 23$

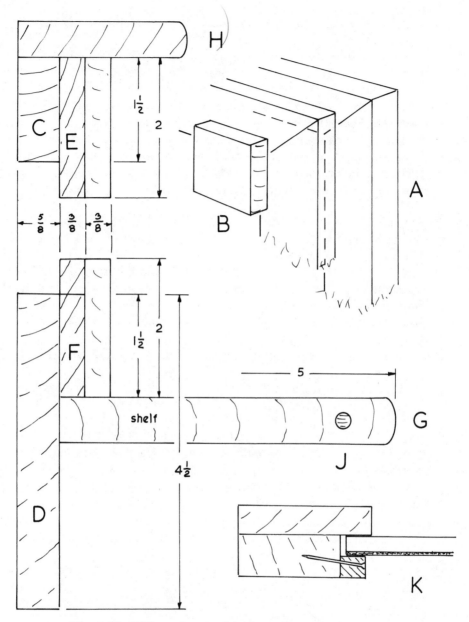

Fig. 4-21. Sections of parts of the frame for a mirror or picture.

1. Prepare wood to the sections for the frame with a few inches extra on the lengths.
2. Cut the back pieces (FIG. 4-21C and D) first. Miter the corners with the inside measurements to suit the glass to be enclosed. Miter the wide bottom piece to match the others (FIG. 4-20A).

3. Glue on the pieces that form the front (FIG. 4-21E and F). See that the parts are assembled parallel.
4. Cut the miters on the front pieces with the back parts as a guide. Try the frame together. See that opposite sides are parallel and that the miters fit reasonably.
5. Join the parts made so far. The miters can be glued and a fine nail driven each way. Leave the assembly back-down on a flat surface.
6. Make the 2-inch square corner pieces and glue them in position (FIGS. 4-20B and 21B). Make sure the inner edges match. If the outer edges need trimming, plane them after assembly. Check the squareness of outer edges and that the extended part of the bottom back piece continues down the line of the sides.
7. Prepare the shelf (FIGS. 4-20C and 21G) to a length matching the bottom of the frame and with a rounded front edge. Drill the back for a few screws, but do not yet join on the shelf.
8. Make the pair of sides (FIG. 4-20D). Lightly round the front edges. These are shown with straight front edges, but you can shape them, as well as the front of the shelf.
9. Make the top (FIG. 4-20E and 21H) so it overhangs at the front and sides. Round its exposed edges.
10. Glue the shelf under the projecting part of the frame and screw through the back into it.
11. Add the sides with glue and a few pins, punched below the surface and covered with stopping. If the shelf is expected to carry much weight, you can include a 1/4-inch dowel to the side at each end (FIG. 4-21J).
12. Glue and pin on the top to complete assembly.
13. Check that the mirror or picture and its backing will fit, but complete finishing with stain and polish before securing in position.
14. A mirror can be backed by a piece of card, with fillets lightly pinned all around to hold it in place (FIG. 4-21K). A picture behind glass can be backed with hardboard or thin plywood with pins directly behind it at intervals. In both cases the mirror or picture can be removed by withdrawing pins.
15. You can hang the unit with a pair of metal plates extending from the sides near the top. You can drill through the frame within a few inches of the top for screws. An additional screw can be positioned under the shelf.

Hanging Caddy

Cupboards and cabinets do not necessarily have doors hinged on vertical edges. Sometimes it is better to arrange the doors to swing upwards or downwards. One advantage of a dropping door or flap is it can be supported horizontally, making it a work surface or somewhere to put things as you take them from the cupboard. The flap can serve as a writing surface. These advantages are as useful today as they were in earlier days.

This reproduction of a wall caddy (FIG. 4-22) has a main compartment with a front door that swings out to horizontal. When closed, it is held in position by the lid, which can be swung up, allowing good access to the interior. Below the main compartment is another one with a pair of small doors, which swing out to act as supports for the flap. The caddy has uses in a kitchen or garage. In a hall it can keep gloves, scarves and other small items tidy and available. Near a telephone the caddy can provide storage for directories and papers, as well as serve as a desk for writing notes.

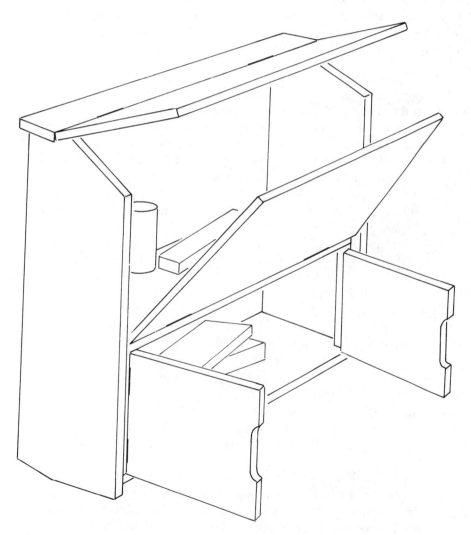

Fig. 4-22. This hanging caddy has a door which forms a flap.

2 sides	$5/8 \times$	7	$\times$	21
2 shelves	$5/8 \times$	6	$\times$	18
1 top	$5/8 \times$	$2^{1}/2 \times$		19
1 lid	$5/8 \times$	7	$\times$	19
1 flap	$5/8 \times$	9	$\times$	18
2 doors	$5/8 \times$	6	$\times$	9
1 back	$1/4 \times$	16	$\times$	20 plywood

If you make the caddy to the sizes shown (FIG. 4-23), you can use $5/8$-inch wood throughout, except for the plywood back. For normal indoor use a hardwood that can be finished with stain and polish should be used, but painted softwood can be used in some situations. The shelves are dowelled to the sides, but dado joints can be used. Hinges can all be 2 inches long.

1. Mark out the pair of sides (FIGS. 4-23A and 24A). Draw on the shelf positions (FIG. 4-25A). The edges should be $3/4$ inch back from the front edges of the sides, to give clearance for the $5/8$ inch thickness of the doors. Rabbet the rear edges to suit the plywood back. Cut the beveled ends.
2. Make the two shelves (FIG. 4-24B) the same size. They control the width of the caddy. Mark the shelf ends and the caddy sides for dowels. For $5/8$-inch wood they can be $3/8$ inch diameter.
3. Have the back plywood (FIG. 4-24C) ready, then join the shelves to the sides with glued dowels and pin or screw on the back with glue to hold the assembly square.
4. Put strips between the shelves at both sides (FIGS. 4-23B and 25B). These provide hinge points for the lower pair of doors. Put a strip of similar section under the upper shelf (FIG. 4-24D). This is needed to give clearance for the main flap when lowered.
5. Put a strip down the top edge of each side, stopping $5/8$ inch from the front (FIG. 4-25C), to stiffen the top and act as a stop for the front flap.
6. Make the top (FIG. 4-24E) and the lid (FIG. 4-24F) so it overhangs the sides by $1/4$ inch. The lid should be 1 inch over the front edge. Bevel the meeting edges so the joint fits closely. Round the outer edges and corners. Screw the top to the sides.
7. Fit the flap between the sides with enough clearance to allow easy movement. Its lower edges should be level with the underside of the shelf. Its top edge should be beveled to match the slope of the lid, and fit closely under it.
8. Do not put the pair of bottom doors directly under the flap, but fit them inside the strip framing. This allows them to swing out under the lowered flap and support it. You can fit handles, but the doors are shown with finger gaps (FIGS. 4-23D and 24G). Put a small block under the center of the strip below the shelf to act as a stop when the doors are closed.

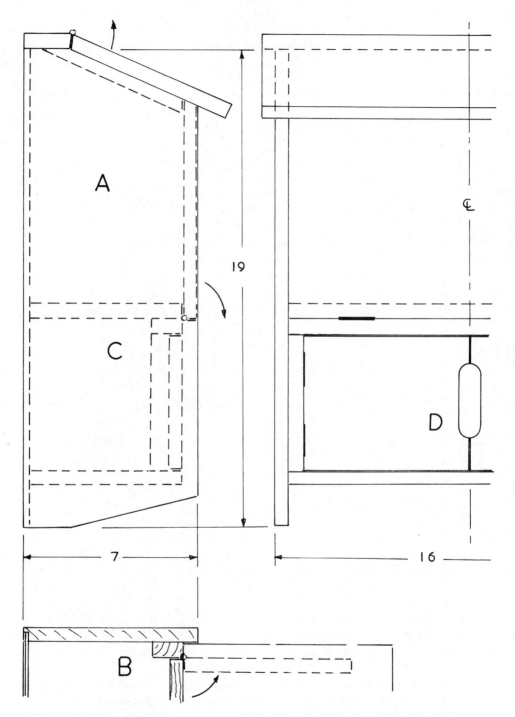

Fig. 4-23. Sizes of the hanging wall caddy.

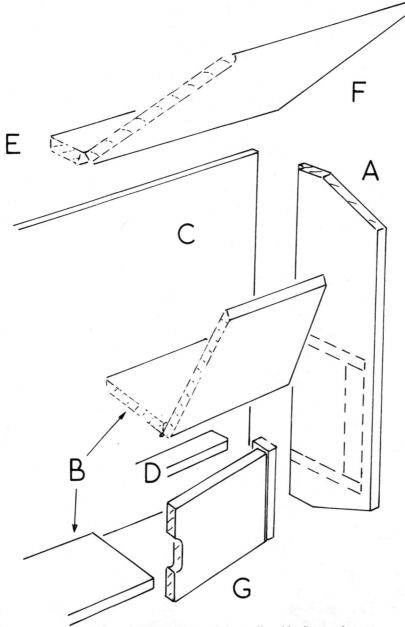

Fig. 4-24. How parts of the wall caddy fit together.

9. Two hinges at each pivoting position are sufficient. Let the hinges into the edges so only a slight clearance exists when the hinges are closed.
10. Assemble the parts with the hinges in position to check action. You will probably have to ease door and flap edges to get neat and parallel closures.

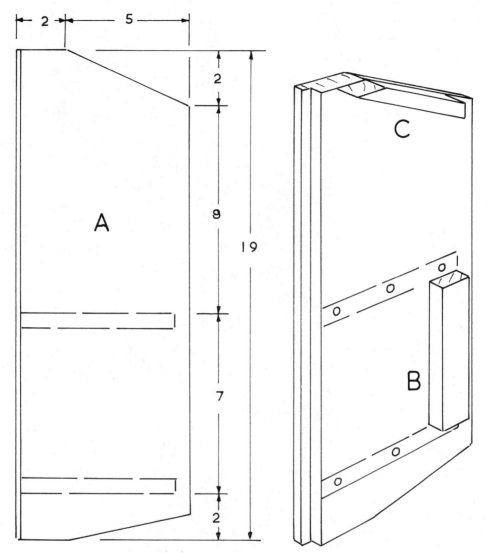

Fig. 4-25. Details of a side of the hanging wall caddy.

11. Take off the doors, flap, and lid. Round the finger grips on the doors. Take off sharpness of all exposed edges. Sand all over and apply your chosen finish, then screw the hinged parts together again.

12. Mount the caddy with screws through the back. Two widely spaced screws near the top should take the weight, but you can also put at least one more near the bottom.

5

Racks and stands

When early homes were set up, there was a great need for furniture to lift such things as clothing and crockery off the floor—which may have been just earth—so there are many original racks and stands on which to base reproductions. Even if we don't have a dirt floor, we still might want many things lifted to convenient heights. These light pieces of furniture, made similarly to the early pieces, are still welcomed for modern use.

Modern versions might use plywood and prepared dowel rods, but these materials were not available to the early woodworkers, so in some projects you may have to decide if you want to follow the original concept closely, or if utility or ease of construction is more important. Although many original racks and stands were made of fairly thick wood, because of problems in converting logs to thin boards and the risk of warping or splitting of poorly seasoned wood, you may decide to lighten appearance by using thinner wood in some situations. The authentic country furniture look, however, does come partly from the strong, rigid appearance of wood a little thicker than might be found in modern furniture.

Quilt or Drying Rack

There are several possible ways of arranging horizontal rails to support quilts or blankets or to act as drying racks for towels and similar things. This rack (FIG. 5-1) has shaped solid wood ends that support three high rails. The two lower rails provide stiffness, but they can be used as a shoe rack or to support a bowl or basket used to transport washing.

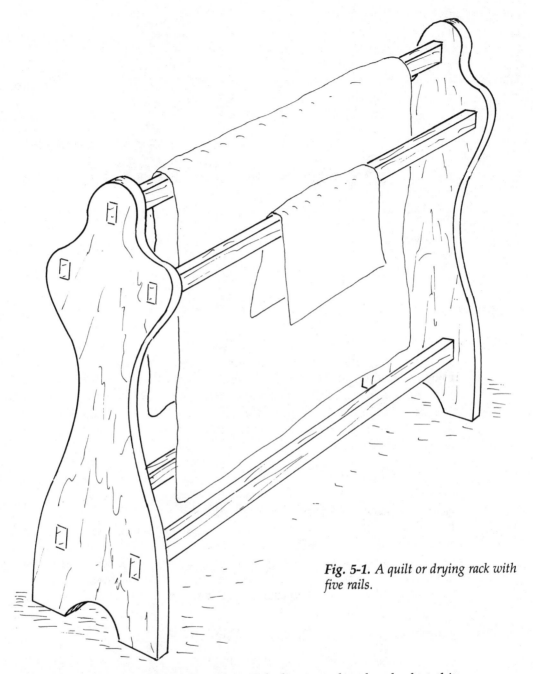

Fig. 5-1. A quilt or drying rack with five rails.

A similar rack could be made with 1-inch-diameter dowel rods, but this design calls for rails in 1-inch by 1½-inch sections with rounded corners and tenons into the ends to ensure a very rigid assembly.

Although it would be possible to use softwood for the rack and finish it with paint, hardwood with a clear finish looks attractive in any surroundings. Choose wood with reasonably straight grain for the rails, but a twisted grain pattern can add an interesting appearance to the ends.

As drawn (FIG. 5-2), the rack is 34 inches high and long, with a width of 12 inches. The lengths of rails can be altered without affecting construction. The rail sections should be stiff enough up to 50 inches long.

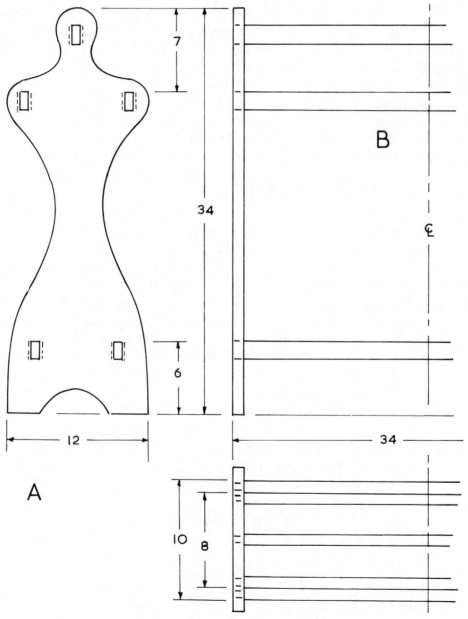

Fig. 5-2. *Suggested sizes for the quilt or drying rack.*

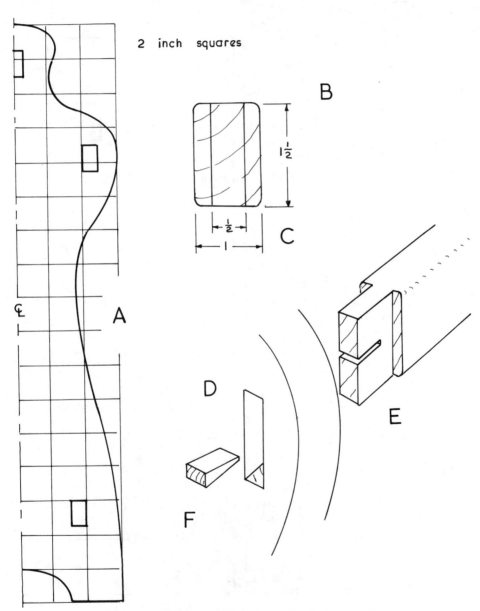

2 inch squares

Fig. 5-3. Shape and joint details for the quilt rack.

1. Mark out the pair of ends (FIG. 5-2A) using a squared drawing (FIG. 5-3A) to work each side of a centerline. Locate all the mortise positions, but it is wiser not to cut the mortises and the outlines until the rails are prepared.
2. The five rails (FIG. 5-2B) are all the same, so mark them together to get the lengths identical.
3. Lightly round the corners (FIG. 5-3B).
4. Mark the tenons 1/2 inch thick (FIG. 5-3C) and long enough to go through the ends with a little to spare.
5. Cut mortises in the ends to match the tenons (FIG. 5-3D).
6. Cut the outlines of the ends. Remove all saw marks and take sharpness off edges.
7. Make saw cuts across the ends of the tenons (FIG. 5-3E) and cut wedges to tighten the joints (FIG. 5-3F). It is sufficient to put a single wedge in each tenon, but for extra strength you can arrange two wedges, evenly spaced, if you consider it necessary.
8. In an original construction the parts were put together without glue, but you should use glue. Check squareness as you assemble. See that the rack stands upright on a level surface. Leave the wedges projecting until the glue sets, then plane the wedges and the tenon ends level.
9. Remove any excess glue. Sand all over and then apply your chosen finish.

Plant Stand

When candles were the main means of illumination, it was important to get this rather feeble source of light into the most favorable position. Often this was done with stands that could be positioned beside a chair or anywhere light was needed. We may not have this problem now, but such a stand can be used for a table lamp. A more interesting use is as a support for a display of flowers in a vase, or a plant in a pot.

Candle stands were made in great variety, from quite crude assemblies to elaborate pieces of furniture. This candle or plant stand (FIG. 5-4) is made like a tall three-legged table. Besides the top there is a shelf which braces the legs and serves as a support for a second floral display or pot plant. Three legs will stand without wobbling on any surface, so besides its use indoors this stand can be used on the ground outdoors.

Construction is quite light. Rigidity depends on accurate, tight-fitting joints. Hardwood or softwood can be used, but if the stand is to take its place among other indoor furniture, you will want to use a matching wood and finish. Use a waterproof glue, preferably of a boatbuilding type, to withstand possible wet conditions—even an overflowing vase indoors.

The suggested sizes (FIG. 5-5A) can be altered to suit your needs, but you will have to follow through the layout instructions using the new measurements. Allow ample spread at the feet to keep the stand stable against normal knocks.

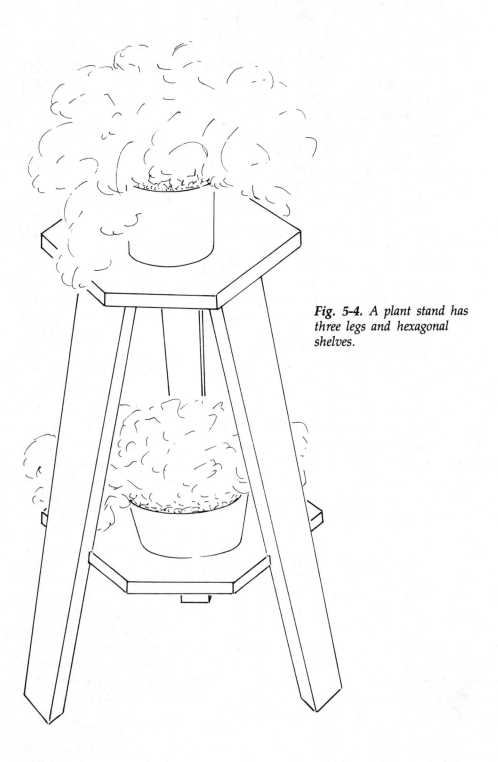

Fig. 5-4. A plant stand has three legs and hexagonal shelves.

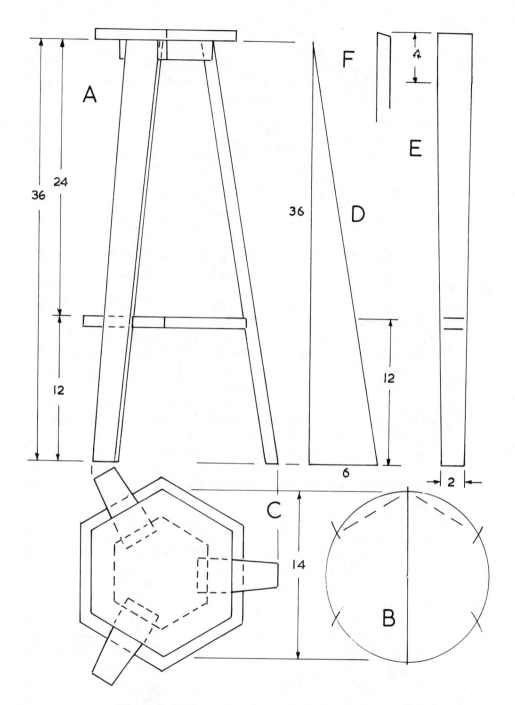

Fig. 5-5. *Sizes and the way to set out the plant stand.*

Marking out relies on drawing regular hexagons. This is done by marking outlines at 60°, but the sizes given are across the points, so it is easier to use circles. Draw a circle equal in diameter to the distance between the points of the hexagon, then step off the radius around the circle. It will go six times (FIG. 5-5B). Join these crossings to obtain your regular hexagon.

Materials List for Plant Stand

1 top	3/4 × 14 × 14	
1 shelf	3/4 × 16 × 16	
1 block	1 1/2 × 10 × 10	
3 legs	1 × 3 × 39	

1. Mark out and cut the hexagonal top (FIG. 5-5C) 14 inches across the points.
2. Mark out and cut the shelf in a similar way 16 inches across the points (FIG. 5-6A).
3. Mark out and cut the hexagonal outline of the thicker block 10 inches across the points (FIG. 5-6B). Do not cut the recesses yet.
4. To obtain the slope and length of the legs, draw a triangle (FIG. 5-5D). On this mark the shelf's height. Set an adjustable bevel to the angle between the leg slope and a horizontal line. This gives you you the angles of meeting parts.
5. Mark out and cut the three legs (FIG. 5-5E). Obtain the length from the triangle and mark on the position of the shelf. Keep each leg 3 inches parallel for the top 4 inches, then taper to 2 inches wide. Bevel top (FIG. 5-5F) and bottom to the angle obtained from the triangle.
6. Mark notches in three sides of the block to match the widths of the legs and to the depths of their tops (FIG. 5-6C). Cut the bottoms of the notches to suit the slopes of the legs.
7. Cut grooves across at the shelf positions (FIG. 5-6D). Keep the grooves less than halfway through the legs, but make them all the same.
8. Drill the legs for two screws at each crossing—#8 gauge by 2 inch is a suitable size. Allow for the heads going below the surface so they can be covered with stopping (FIG. 5-6E).
9. Take sharpness off all exposed edges and sand parts that will be inaccessible after assembly.
10. Glue and screw the legs to the block and to the shelf. Try the assembly on a level surface and view it from all angles before the glue sets. The assembly should tighten to a symmetrical shape, but make sure the block is parallel to the floor and the angles of the legs are the same.
11. The shelf joints can be reinforced with blocks glued below (FIG. 5-6F). They should match the widths of the legs.

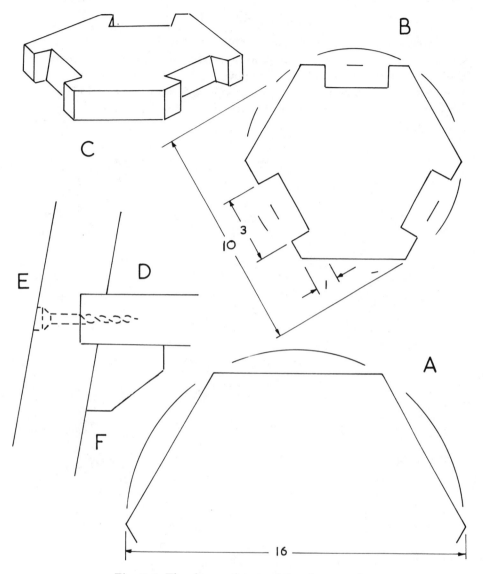

Fig. 5-6. The shapes of parts of the plant stand.

12. Level the tops of the legs and the block, then glue the stand top in position. If the block and top grains cross they will help each other resist warping. You can drill three widely-spaced screws downwards from the top into the block.

13. Finish the stand to suit the wood. On surfaces where pots or vases will stand there should not be too high a gloss.

Two-Tier Book Trough

This project is a rack for two rows of books and is designed so the books are angled to make them easier to see and more accessible than if the shelves were level (FIG. 5-7). It is assumed that the books on the lower trough will be 7 inches by 9 inches and those on the top trough will be 5 inches by 8 inches, but other size books can be accommodated. You may make the shelves different lengths to suit space of the number of books.

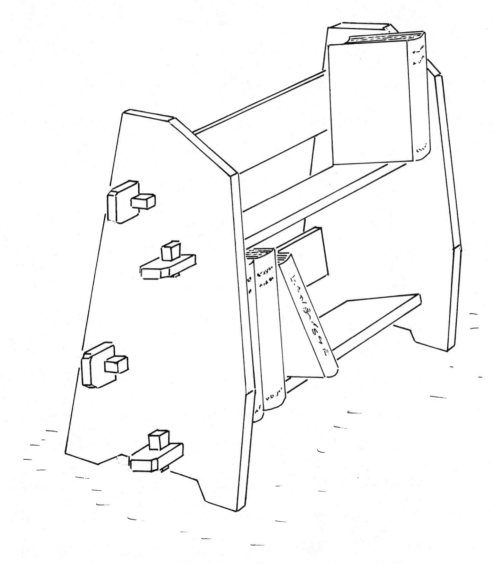

Fig. 5-7. A two-tier book trough with wedged tenon joints.

As drawn (FIG. 5-8), the trough is suitable for standing on a table. If you want it to stand on the floor, extend the sides downward to make longer feet. The slopes of the troughs will give you a good view of the books without having to stoop.

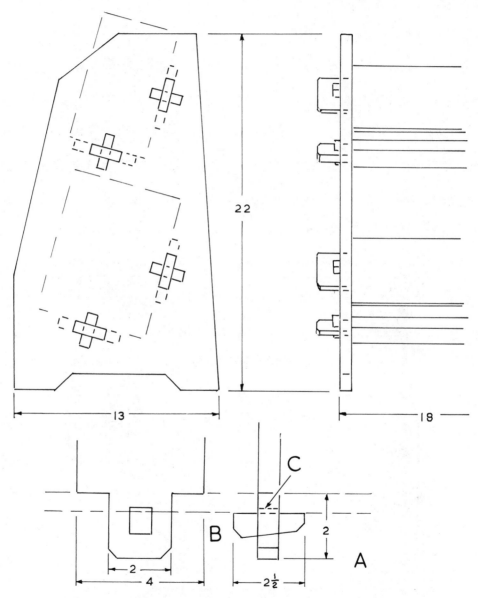

Fig. 5-8. Sizes and joint details of the two-tier book trough.

The two-tier book trough is best made with good furniture-quality hardwood. The pressure of the wedges on the end-grain of the tenons might be too much for softwood. In any case, books look best against polished hardwood.

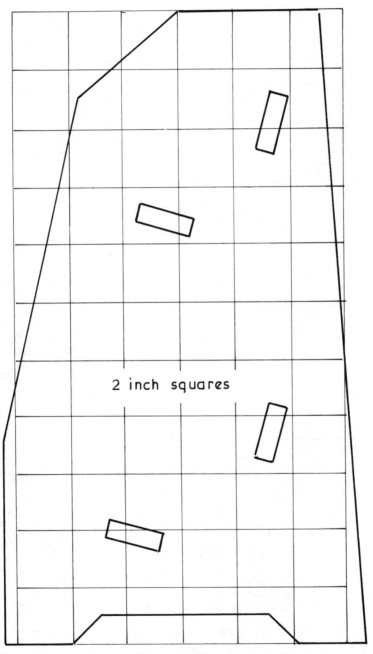

2 inch squares

Fig. 5-9. Layout of the end of the two-tier book trough.

Materials List for
Two-Tier Book Trough

2 sides	$5/8$ × 13 × 24	
4 shelves	$5/8$ ×	4 × 24

1. The books are tilted at 15° to horizontal. The mortises for the shelves are all 2 inches wide. Set out the pair of ends (FIG. 5-9). It is helpful to draw a centerline and relate the mortises to that. Make sure the lower mortises are both at the same angle, then draw the rear mortises square to the lower mortises—otherwise the angles will not match the 90° angles of the corners of books.
2. Cut the outlines of the ends, but leave the mortises until you have the tenons ready to match them.
3. Mark all four shelves together so they are the same, allowing them to fit in any position if you re-assemble the trough.
4. Cut the tenons to go 2 inches through the sides (FIG. 5-8A). Bevel the outer corners. Cut the mortises in the sides to match the tenons.
5. Cut the wedges from $3/4$-inch-square strip. Make each wedge about $1/2$ inch too long at first. This allows you to trim the ends evenly after a trial assembly. Mark a wedge on the end of a strip. Plane the taper to $9/16$ inch, then cut the wedge off and make the others, using the first as a guide so they are uniform (FIG. 5-8B).
6. Cut the wedge holes so the inner edge is $1/16$ inch within the thickness of the side (FIG. 5-8C). Bevel the outer side of each hole so it matches the slope of the wedges.
7. Try the parts together. Trim the wedges so they project equal amounts on each side of their tenon. Bevel or round the ends of the wedges.
8. Take the trough apart. Take the sharpness off all edges or lightly round the shelf edges and the parts of the sides which are upwards.
9. Sand all over and finish with stain and polish before making the final assembly.

Corner Stand

A corner stand, or "whatnot," once held family treasures or floral displays. Such a stand still has uses in the corner of a room, where space is not otherwise filled. It can be used for flowers or plants, or it can be a place to put papers and magazines in a den.

This stand (FIG. 5-10) has three shelves of graduated sizes, supported on four uprights which can be screwed to the wall or left free-standing. The stand is shown with little decoration, but the outer edges can be molded, although that was unlikely in original Colonial days. If the stand will display flowers or plants, they should provide all the decoration required.

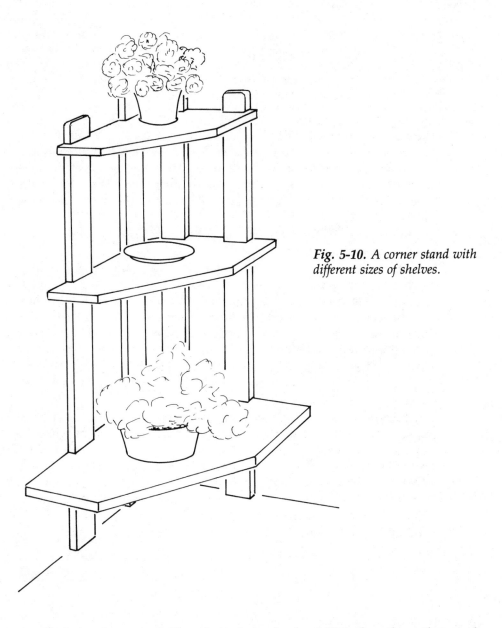

Fig. 5-10. *A corner stand with different sizes of shelves.*

As drawn (FIG. 5-11A), the whatnot stands about 12 inches above the usual table height. The top shelf extends from the corner about 12 inches. The other shelves are 2 inches and 4 inches wider. You may want to check these sizes against the corner where the whatnot will stand. Variations in size need not alter the method of construction. Do not make the shelves too narrow, as the diagonal arrangement may not give you much useful flat area.

Room corners are not always square. If you want to fit the stand into a particular corner, try a square in the corner about 30 inches from the floor. If the corner

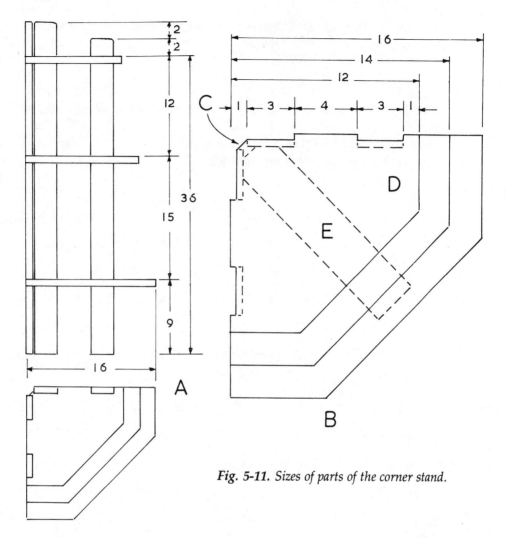

Fig. 5-11. Sizes of parts of the corner stand.

angle is very far from 90°, set an adjustable bevel to the actual angle and use this instead of a square when marking the shelves. A template as large as the biggest shelf can be cut and used to mark out shelves. If the unit will be free-standing, or if it will be available for different corners, you will have to settle for 90°.

**Materials List for
Corner Stand**

1 shelf	3/4 × 15 × 24	
1 shelf	3/4 × 13 × 22	
1 shelf	3/4 × 11 × 20	
2 legs	3/4 × 3 × 40	
2 legs	3/4 × 3 × 42	

1. Mark out the large shelf first (FIG. 5-11B). Have the grain of all shelves diagonal to the corner. If you set out the positions of the uprights on the underside of the shelf, this can be used as a guide when marking the other two shelves.
2. At the uprights there are halved joints, with 3/8 inch cut from the shelf to fit into the other parts and come level with the rear edges of the uprights (FIG. 5-12A). At the corners, cut across between the joints (FIGS. 5-11C and 12B). Room corners may not be sharp, and cutting the shelves away keeps them clear of possible difficulty in fitting.

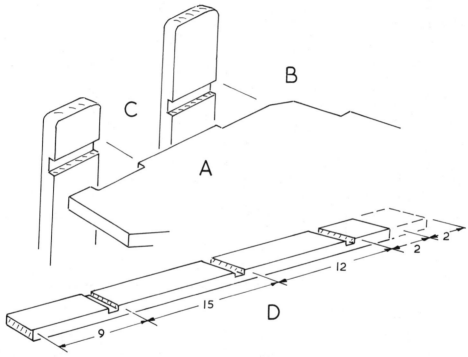

Fig. 5-12. Support details for the corner stand.

3. Cut the two smaller shelves to shape (FIG. 5-11D). Reduce them in 2 inch steps, but make the corners and the notches for the uprights the same as on the large shelf.
4. The wood may be stiff enough to resist warping, but because the bottom shelf extends cross-grained some way from the support of the uprights it should be strengthened by a diagonal brace (FIG. 5-11E) screwed underneath to guard against cracking or warping. Use screws without glue so a little expansion and contraction can take place without causing problems. A similar piece can be put under the next shelf. If the front of the braces are tapered they will not be visible from a normal viewing angle.

5. The four uprights are the same, except the rear ones extend 2 inches above the others. Mark them together. Cut the grooves halfway through the wood and make them fit closely on the shelves (FIG. 5-12C and D).
6. The tops of the uprights are shown rounded, but you can use other shaping or can mold them and the shelf edges to match.
7. Join the uprights to the shelves with glue and two screws driven from the back at each joint. Try the unit in the corner if it is to be fitted in a particular place. Otherwise, see that the parts are square to each other and the legs stand without wobbling on a flat floor.
8. Finish the wood with stain and polish or paint. If the stand will be secured in place, it is probably sufficient to drive screws through the two outer uprights inconspicuously under the middle shelf.

Display Rack

This three-shelf display rack or stand (FIG. 5-13) is arranged so the lower shelves project in front of those above, and there is space for tall plants or other display items of any height. Each shelf has a back and there is a bar directly above it below the next shelf, so plates or other items stood on edge can rest there. The backs and bars also add strength, providing rigidity in the length of the rack. The supports are frames built up from strips halved together.

What is displayed on the rack should provide decoration and eye appeal. The rack is only background, so it is not designed to be decorative itself. For a floral and plant display, it can be made of softwood and painted, although it can be left untreated for use outdoors. For indoors use, the whole rack can be made of hardwood, or an attractive hardwood with a clear finish can be used for the shelves, backs and bars. The supporting frame can be made of softwood painted in a neutral color.

Sizes are suggested (FIG. 5-14), but they can be altered. If you want to make the rack much longer, include a third supporting framework.

**Materials List for
Display Rack**

2 uprights	1 × 2 × 34
2 uprights	1 × 2 × 25
2 uprights	1 × 2 × 14
2 rails	1 × 2 × 16
2 rails	1 × 2 × 10
2 rails	1 × 2 × 8
2 feet	1 × 3 × 24
3 shelves	1 × 7 × 44
3 shelf backs	1 × 3 × 44
3 shelf bars	1 × 2 × 44
1 back rail	1 × 3 × 34

Fig. 5-13. *A display rack with stepped shelves.*

1. Prepare the wood for all parts. Most sizes of sections are interrelated. If your 1-inch by 2-inch strips actually finish $7/8$-inch by $17/8$-inch section it doesn't matter, but you must allow for this when marking and cutting joints. Similarly, shelves need not be exactly to the specified sections, but when marking out the framing you must allow for the actual widths.
2. Each frame (FIG. 5-14A) consists of three uprights and three rails, with the uprights attached to a base (FIG. 5-15A). Mark out the numbered pieces (FIG. 5-16A). At each position, mark the actual width of the crossing piece

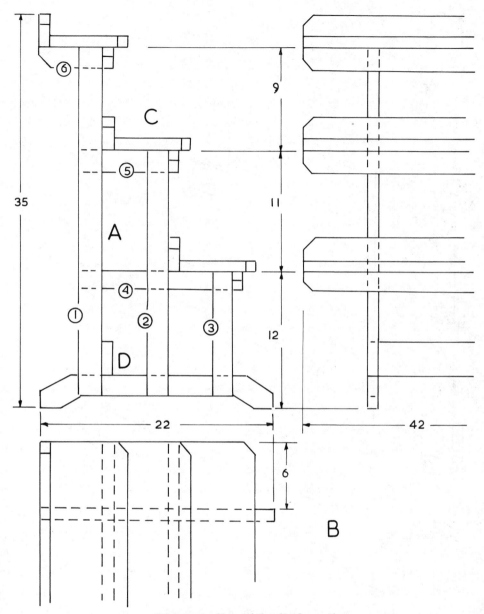

Fig. 5-14. Sizes of the display rack.

and square down the edges to give the outline of the halving joint (FIG. 5-16B).

3. Mark out the bases (FIGS. 5-15B and 16C). Make sure the positions of the halving joints match those on the rail above. Cut the outline of each base so there are feet and the depth to be halved is 2 inches.

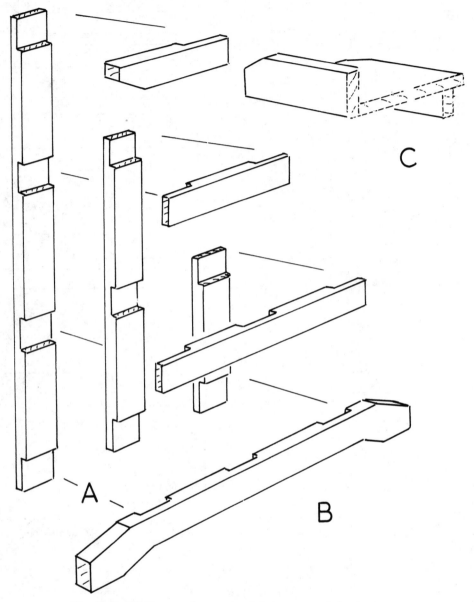

Fig. 5-15. Fitting together parts of the support of the display rack.

4. Cut all the halving joints. Join them with glue and one screw in the middle of each joint. Make sure the parts go together squarely and the two assemblies match each other. Level any projecting ends and remove excess glue.
5. Make the shelves (FIG. 5-16D). Mark the positions of the frames underneath and cut off the front corners (FIG. 5-14B).

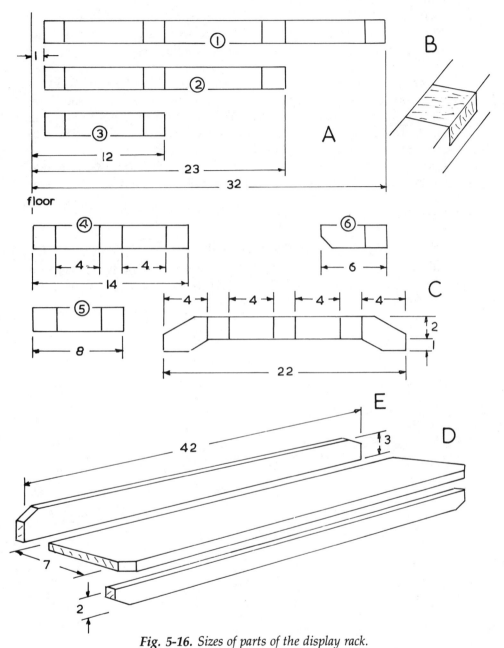

Fig. 5-16. *Sizes of parts of the display rack.*

6. The backs of the shelves (FIG. 5-16E) should be glued and screwed to the rear edges of the shelves and have matching cutoff corners.

7. Fit the bars underneath (FIG. 5-15C). They should be 1 inch back from the front of their shelf, but the shelf assemblies must fit over the steps in

the frames. Check each shelf assembly in the position it will go and locate the bars underneath so they and the shelf backs come against the uprights (FIG. 5-14C). This is important for secure screwing at both positions.

8. Prepare the shelves to screw into the frames. At each crossing three screws should go through the shelf and one should be drilled in each of the vertical pieces. You may just countersink and drive screw heads level with the surface in some situations. For a better finish, the screws can be counterbored and the sunk heads covered with wood plugs—#8 or 10 gauge by 2-inch screws are suitable.

9. Assemble the shelves to the frames, checking squareness as you progress.

10. See that the assembly stands level. Put a rail (FIG. 5-14D) across the rear uprights.

11. Finish to suit the wood and the situation.

Turned Stand

Many early candle stands were turned, and this smaller version is suitable for a potted plant or vase of flowers (FIG. 5-17). Your lathe must be able to swing a 12-

Fig. 5-17. This stand is made completely on a lathe.

inch diameter disc over the bed or in an outboard position and be able to take 24 inches between centers.

Use a stable hardwood free from flaws. Saw the discs close to size, but you should be able to turn the spindle directly from square stock.

Materials List for
Turned Stand

1 spindle	$2^1/2$ ×	$2^1/2$ × 24	
1 top	$1^1/4$ ×	10	× 10
1 top	$1^1/4$ ×	6	× 6
1 bottom	$1^1/4$ ×	12	× 12
1 bottom	$1^1/4$ ×	7	× 7
3 feet	$1^1/2$ ×	3	× 3

1. Turn the spindle first (FIG. 5-18A). You can use your own ideas for a pattern, but the one shown is similar to an original and has a pleasing appearance. The largest diameter is $2^1/2$ inches. The beads at the ends (FIG. 5-18B) should be 2 inches diameter and the dowels could be 1 inch diameter. Make a hole in a piece of scrap wood, using the bit that will drill the discs, and fit the dowels to that. At both ends the dowel should go through the first disc and a short distance into the next one, to ensure the parts assembling concentrically (FIG. 5-18C).

2. Turn the disc that goes under the top (FIG. 5-18D). Use a plain profile because normally this part will not be visible. Drill right through its center.

3. Turn the smaller bottom disc (FIG. 5-18E) in a similar way. Its edge and that of the larger disc should have similar sections to give a matching molded appearance.

4. Make the top (FIG. 5-18F) with a hollowed surface, but take care to keep its bottom flat across. Drill centrally in the bottom surface deep enough to take the end of the spindle dowel.

5. Keep the top surface of the larger bottom disc flat (FIG. 5-18G), so it fits closely against the other one, and turn a complementary edge. Drill for the tip of the spindle dowel in the same way as at the top.

6. Turn the feet with $1/2$-inch dowels projecting to fit into holes in the base (FIG. 5-18H). Make sure the feet are all the same thickness.

7. For greatest stability, the feet edges should be level with the outside of the base disc. Draw a pitch circle for the dowel holes (FIG. 5-18J) that puts them in the right position. Step off the radius around the circle to find the three hole positions.

8. Some parts might be stained and polished while in the lathe, but it probably is better to apply a finish after gluing the parts together. Discs of cloth can be glued under the feet to prevent slipping.

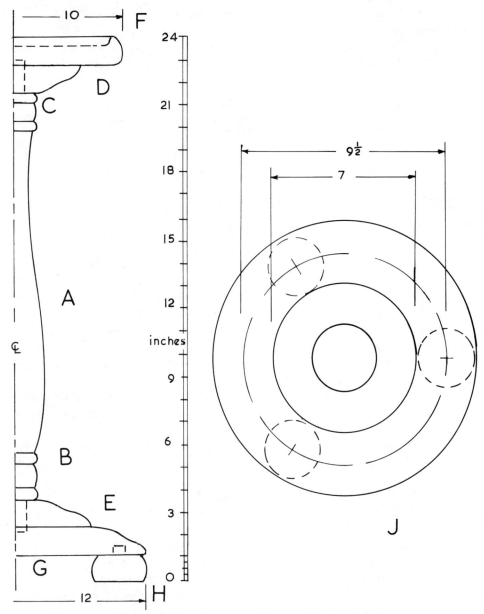

Fig. 5-18. Sizes and layout of the turned stand.

6

Tables and cabinets

Many traditional kinds of tables involve more work than can be put into a weekend, so they are unsuitable for this book. Others were rather crude. Some of these primitive tables might be used outdoors, but you are unlikely to want them in the house. Similarly, the many cabinets, hutches, cupboards, and other enclosed pieces of furniture may involve more work than can be accomplished in one weekend.

By having everything ready and tackling the work in an orderly fashion, you might be able to accomplish more than you thought possible, but tables and cabinets should be restricted to the more basic patterns. Too much decoration, or a multiplicity of drawers, may make the project a more than one-weekend undertaking. Size need not be a deterrent. A large table need involve no more work than a small one made the same way.

Although dowels were not used much in early tables and cabinets, they can be used so they do not show. You can make neat and strong pieces of furniture by using dowels where early craftsmen might have nailed. For framed parts it is usually stronger to cut mortise and tenon joints.

Slab Table

This simple table (FIG. 6-1) has wide wood slabs for its top and ends. A drawer is provided and there is a foot rail at the back. The table can be made plain as a useful bench for hobby use, but it is shown with the bottoms cut away to form feet and there are heart cutouts large enough to provide hand holes for lifting the table. This can make a dresser in a small bedroom or a table in a hall, if it is under a wall mirror.

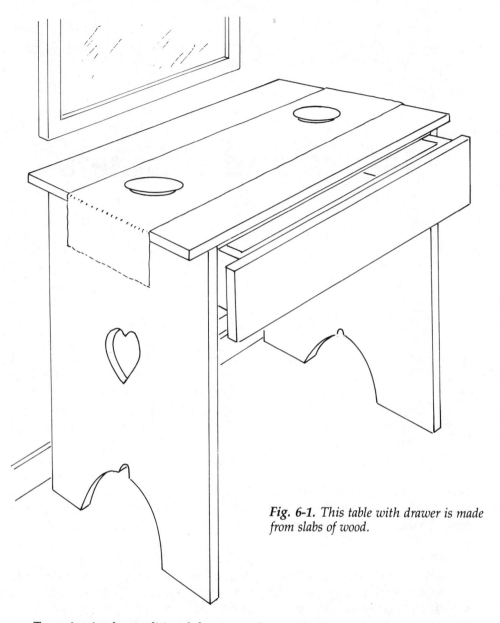

Fig. 6-1. *This table with drawer is made from slabs of wood.*

To maintain the traditional furniture theme, all the parts should be solid wood. You can glue pieces together to make up the widths. If you do not wish to keep too closely to traditional construction, plywood or particleboard veneered to match any solid wood parts can be used. In the instructions and materials list, it is assumed you will use solid wood. Hardwood is advisable and you may choose a local one or wood to match existing furniture. This should be given an appropriate clear finish. You could use softwood and paint it, which might be attractive in a child's room.

There are parts, such as the rails into the ends, where mortise and tenon joints are strongest, but dowels can be used for these and all other joints. Do not drill through boards, but take the dowels as deep as possible without marking the outer surfaces. Use 3/8-inch hardwood dowels, with two in each narrow end, with about a 3 inch spacing longer joints.

The sizes suggested (FIG. 6-2) allow knee room when sitting. If you alter the sizes, make sure you retain adequate clearance below the drawer and its rail. The

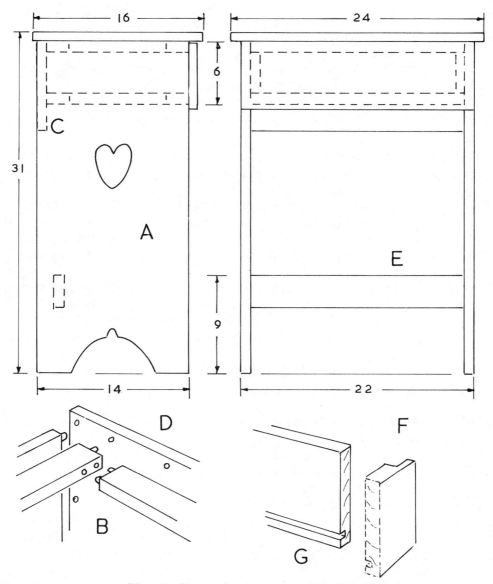

Fig. 6-2. Sizes and construction of the slab table.

drawer front projects a little below the front rail, and you can pull it out by gripping the edge, so there is no need for a knob or handle. You can add one, particularly if you want to match the fronts of other furniture with handles. The top overhangs the back and the drawer front by 1/2 inch and the ends by 1 inch.

Materials List for Slab Table

2 ends	7/8 × 14	× 32	
1 top	7/8 × 16	× 26	
4 frames	1 × 2	× 24	
4 frames	1 × 2	× 16	
1 back	7/8 × 8	× 24	
1 rail	1 × 3	× 24	
2 drawer sides	5/8 × 4	× 16	
1 drawer back	5/8 × 3 1/2	× 24	
1 drawer front	5/8 × 4	× 24	
1 drawer front	5/8 × 6 1/2	× 25	
1 drawer bottom	14 × 22	× 1/4 plywood	

1. Prepare the wood to correct sections. If you glue boards to make up widths, clean off the surplus glue and have these pieces ready to be treated as whole boards.
2. Mark the pair of ends (FIGS. 6-2A and 3A) with the positions of the other parts first. The cutout that forms the feet can be a simple V or curve, but it is shown with a shape compatible with the heart (FIG. 6-4A). The hole can be a curved grip (FIG. 6-4B), but hearts were popular in early furniture and one is appropriate (FIG. 6-4C).
3. The rails above and below the drawer are parts of similar frames (FIG. 6-3B). In each frame the front rail goes across, but the side rails overlap the rear rail, to give a smooth run for the drawer. Front rails are level with the edges of the ends, but allow for the thickness of the back at the rear when cutting the side strips.
4. Join the frame parts with dowels (FIG. 6-2B). They should finish square and the surfaces should be level.
5. Make the back (FIGS. 6-2C and 3C) deeper than the shelf frames, to give rigidity to the table. Prepare the ends, the frames and the table ends for dowel joints (FIG. 6-2D).
6. Cut the foot rail (FIGS. 6-2E and 3D) to the same length as the frames and back. Prepare the ends and the table ends for two or three dowels.
7. Do any sanding or other finishing work on the parts that will be less accessible after assembly.
8. Have sufficient dowels ready, then assemble the crosswise pieces to one side, then add the other. The parts should pull each other square as they are clamped, but check squareness to make sure the table stands firm on a level surface.
9. Make sure the drawer fits before adding the top. You can make the drawer

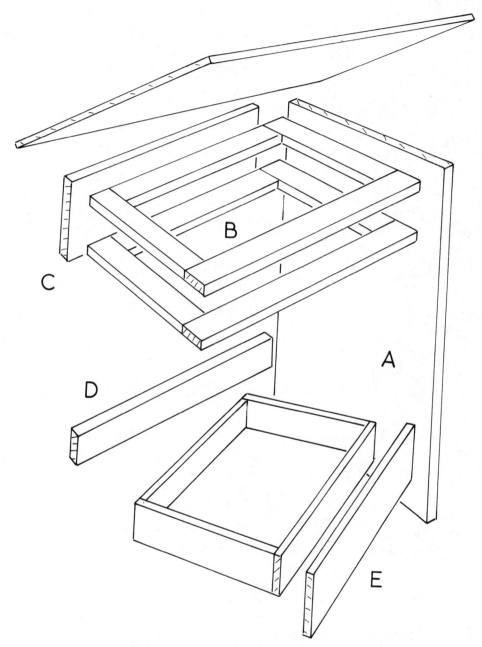

Fig. 6-3. *How parts of the slab table fit together.*

with handcut dovetails in the traditional way, or use half-blind dovetails if you have a suitable router cutter and jig. In a simpler construction, there might be a rabbet in each end on the inner front (FIG. 6-2F), into which the sides may be glued and nailed both ways. Groove the bottom edges for

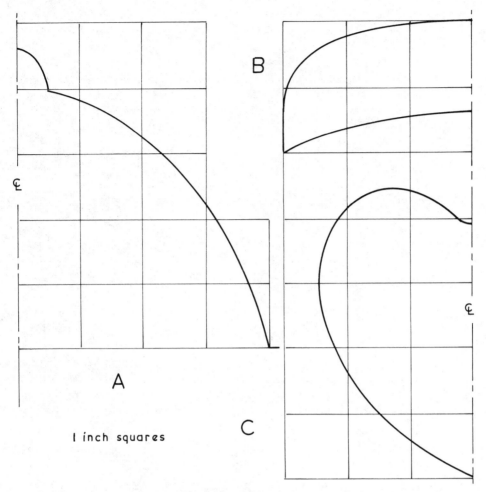

B

A

I inch squares

Fig. 6-4. Shaped parts of the slab table.

thin solid wood, plywood or hardboard (FIG. 6-2G). Make the back to go above the drawer bottom, which can be attached with screws or nails. The drawer should fit into its space with its inner front level with the front of the opening before the drawer reaches the rear of the table. The drawer will be stopped by the outer front fitting close.

10. Make the outer drawer front (FIG. 6-3E) long enough to reach the outside surfaces of the table ends. Its top edge should have about 1/8 inch of clearance under the table top, and its lower edge should come about 1/2 inch below the lower front rail. Round the inner edge of this part to form a comfortable grip.

11. Join the outer front to the drawer with glue and screws from inside. Check the action of the drawer and make any adjustments before adding the table top.

12. Cut the top to size to overhang 1/2 inch at back and front over the drawer and 1 inch at each end. It is shown square-edged, but you can round or mold it if you wish.

13. You can attach the top with screws driven upwards through the top frame, but there is not enough clearance to get a screwdriver in all the places so dowels must be used in some areas. You may prefer to use dowels everywhere, at about 3 inch intervals around the edges of the joining parts.

14. Finish by your chosen method; probably stain and polish.

Standard Tables

Over several centuries four-legged tables have been made in basically the same way. Early settlers needed a substantial table to prepare and eat food and tackle many of the chores incidental to their existence. First tables may have been crudely nailed together, but soon tables with properly jointed parts were made, and that method of construction has continued to the present day, with only minor improvements. Quality of wood, construction and finish may vary according to needs, but the way the tables are made hasn't changed.

Using the same construction methods you can make tables ranging from large dining tables down to side and coffee tables. In its simplest form a table has square legs without taper and a top with square edges. That can serve as a work bench or a dining table to be used with simple chairs. A better table may have tapered or turned legs and a top with molded edges. Good-quality wood with a fine finish might transform a very basic table into something that can take its place with modern furniture.

The first table (FIG. 6-5A) is without embellishments. It can can be made of hardwood and left plain to weather to an old appearance and have its top scrubbed occasionally, or it can be given a stained and clear finish. You might use softwood and paint the lower parts, leaving the top untreated, for occasional scrubbing. Sizes could be anything you wish, but those suggested (FIG. 6-6A) are for a table of moderate size that might be used for eating in a kitchen. If you want to sit at a table using a normal chair, the top must be about 29 inches from the floor and there should be clearance for your knees under the rails.

Despite its plainness, such a table can look attractive if it is nicely proportioned. Keep the three main measurements (length, width and height) obviously different, so far as possible. A top 1 1/2 times as long as it is wide looks better than one nearly square.

Traditional tables had the rails joined to the legs with mortise and tenon joints (FIG. 6-6B). Dowels can be used (FIG. 6-6C), which will not show in the finished table. Carefully fitted mortise and tenon joints are stronger than dowel joints, but if you have doubts about your ability to cut good joints, you might be more successful with dowels. Both methods are described in the instructions.

The method of making the other tables suggested is similar to the first table, and you should refer to the instructions if you make one of the later designs.

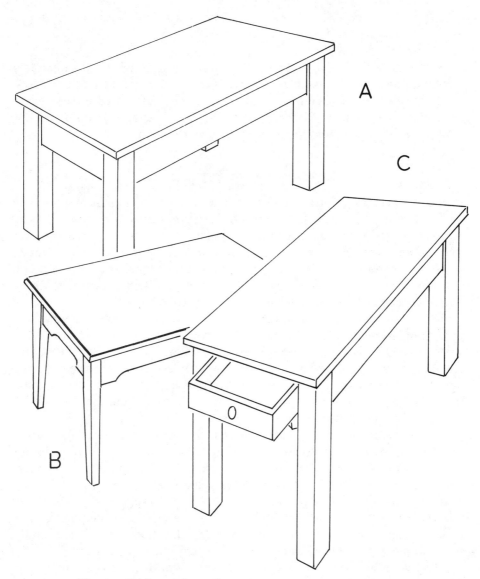

Fig. 6-5. Tables can be made as variations on a standard pattern.

1. Mark all four legs together (FIG. 6-7A), including the locations of mortises (FIG. 6-7B) or dowels (FIG. 6-7C). Square the marks onto an adjoining face and gauge the details of the mortises (FIG. 6-7D) or dowel centers (FIG. 6-7E). If there are any differences in quality of surface or grain markings you favor, make the best sides the unmarked ones so they will be on the outside.

**Materials List
for Standard Tables**

First table

4 legs	$2^1/_2$	×	$2^1/_2$	× 31
2 rails	$7/_8$	×	6	× 30
2 rails	$7/_8$	×	6	× 19
1 top	$7/_8$	×	21	× 36
Buttons from	$3/_4$	×	$1^1/_2$	× 30

Second table

4 legs	$1^3/_4$	×	$1^3/_4$	× 30
2 rails	$7/_8$	×	6	× 28
2 rails	$7/_8$	×	6	× 16
1 top	$7/_8$	×	18	× 32
Buttons from	$3/_4$	×	$1^1/_2$	× 30

Third table

4 legs	$2^1/_2$	×	$2^1/_2$	× 31
2 rails	$7/_8$	×	6	× 30
1 rail	$7/_8$	×	6	× 19
2 rails	$7/_8$	×	2	× 19
Buttons from	$3/_4$	×	$1^1/_2$	× 30
4 drawer guides	$1^1/_8$	×	2	× 18
4 drawer guides	$3/_4$	×	$3/_4$	× 18
1 drawer front	$7/_8$	×	$4^1/_2$	× 16
2 drawer sides	$5/_8$	×	$4^1/_2$	× 18
1 drawer back	$5/_8$	×	4	× 16
1 drawer bottom	$1/_4$	×	14	× 17

2. Mark opposite pairs of rails together (FIG. 6-7F) to ensure they will match. Lengths between shoulders are the important ones if you cut tenons. For doweling, these are the overall lengths.

3. Allow for tenons entering the legs $1^1/_4$ inches (FIG. 6-6D). Make the tenons $1/_2$ inch thick on $7/_8$-inch rails. Mark and cut the tenons as shown (FIGS. 6-6E and 7G).

4. With the tenons as guides, mark the mortises and cut them. Leave a little extra length on the top of each leg, to be trimmed off after assembly.

5. If you choose dowels, they may be $1/_2$ inch diameter. There should be four at each place in $7/_8$ inch wood (FIG. 6-6F). Take them as deep as the tenons (FIG. 6-6G). Make sure the ends of rails are square and that the holes are drilled accurately and are square to the surfaces.

6. A solid-wood top can expand and contract due to humidity. Don't attach the top rigidly to the framework. Plow $1/_4$-by-$1/_4$-inch grooves inside the top edges of the rails (FIG. 6-7H) to take buttons.

7. Make buttons to screw under the top and engage with the grooves (FIG. 6-7J). When the screw is tightened the button lug should pull against the top of the groove.

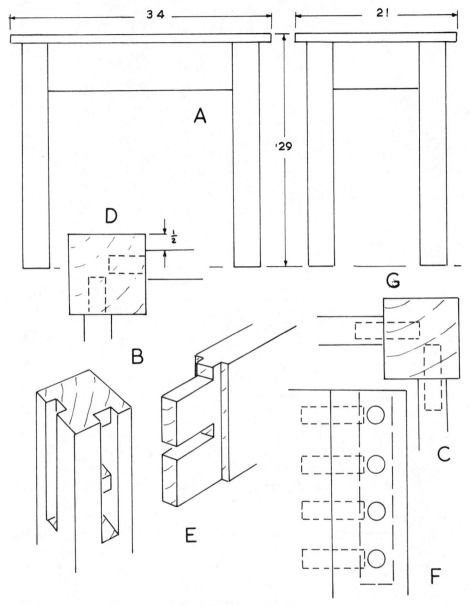

Fig. 6-6. *A standard table with alternative joints.*

8. Cut the bottoms of the legs to length. Bevel them all around to minimize the risk of splintering and to reduce marking of floor coverings.
9. Take sharp edges off all parts that will be exposed. Do any sanding necessary.
10. Assemble in stages. Join rails and legs of opposite long sides first. Check

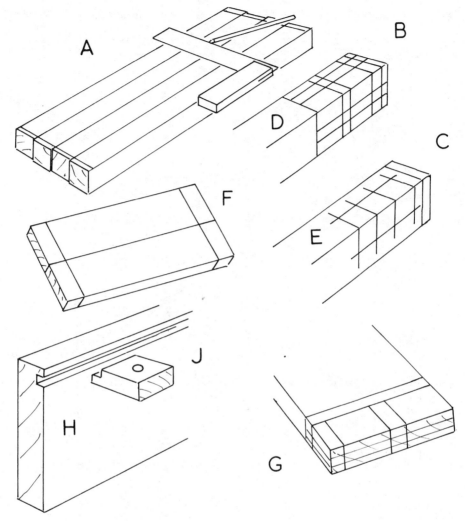

Fig. 6-7. Marking out parts of a standard table.

squareness. See that widths at the feet are the same as at the top. Put one side in its relative position over the other to see they match (FIG. 6-8A). Be careful to make the assemblies without twists.

11. When the glue in these assemblies has set, join them with the rails the other way. Check squareness and that the legs are parallel. Also check squareness as viewed from above (FIG. 6-8B). See that the framework stands level on a flat surface.

12. Remove any surplus glue. Level the tops of the legs with the rails.

13. Make up the width of the top with two or more boards. With a modern glue, it should be sufficient to rely on glue alone if the edges are planed to

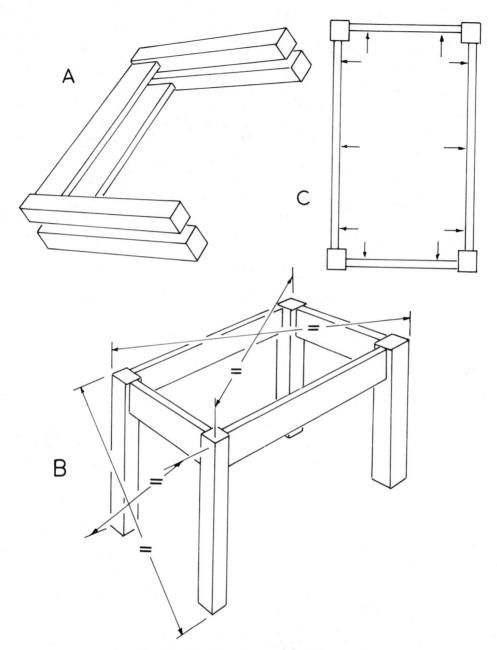

Fig. 6-8. Checking during assembly of a table.

be a good match. With earlier poorer glues, craftsmen had to use dowels
or other ways of increasing the mechanical strength of the joint.
14. Cut the top to size. Square the edges. Lightly round the corners.

15. Invert the framework on the underside of the top. Check that the overhang is the same all around and mark the position.
16. The number of buttons depends on the size of the table, but in this case it should be sufficient to arrange one about 3 inches from the corner along each side and one at the center of each long side (FIG. 6-8C). As you screw on each button, leave a little clearance at the groove to allow for possible expansion and contraction of the top later.
17. Try the completed table on a flat surface. A little may need to come off one leg to make it stand without wobbling.
18. Paint or stain and polish the table.

A lighter and more decorative table can be made using the same construction method. This table (FIGS. 6-5B and 9) is shown in a size suitable for use in writing or serving (FIG. 6-9A). Sizes might be altered to suit your needs. Wood sections are intended for hardwood. They would have to be increased for softwood, but as drawn, the table will look best in an attractive hardwood with a clear finish. The basic construction is the same as just described, but the following instructions allow for variations.

19. Mark the $1^3/4$-inch-square legs with tapers on the inner edges only (FIG. 6-9B). In the finished table the outsides of the legs will be vertical. All the sides can be tapered if you wish, but this would be slight and it is easier to taper two sides only. Do not cut the tapers until after the joints have been prepared.
20. The rails can be tenoned or dowelled. Reduce the rail widths 3 inches from the legs (FIG. 6-9C). Elliptical curves, rather than parts of circles, look better. Make a small template so all the curves are the same.
21. Because the legs are a smaller section, tenons or dowels should be cut to meet so there is adequate glue area. Cut mortises or dowel holes into each other and miter the tenon or dowel ends (FIG. 6-9D). Make sure they are not so long that they meet before the rails' shoulders have pulled tight.
22. Taper the legs and groove the rails for buttons. Prepare the parts for joining, then assemble in the same way as the first table.
23. Make the top 1 inch larger all around (FIG. 6-9E). Mold the top edge. Any pattern for which you have equipment can be used, but early tables had simple moldings or rounded edges.
24. Join the framework to the top with buttons in the way described for the first table. Finish the way you choose.

The usefulness of any table increases by adding a drawer, which can be at one end or in the side. If you want a drawer in one side, make crosswise supports and cut an opening in the way described for fitting a drawer in the Mayflower Stool (FIG. 2-7). Making a relatively small drawer like this does not affect the strength of the table parts enough to matter. If a drawer is put in one or both ends, and you make its width from leg to leg, you

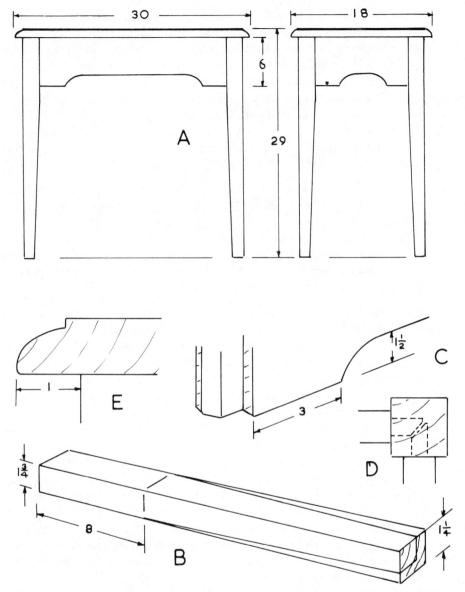

Fig. 6-9. Details of a table with tapered legs and molded top.

have to ensure ample strength in the parts that fit between the legs, otherwise the table will soon lose rigidity. An end drawer can go into the table as far as you wish. It will slide without trouble if the distance into the table is greater than its width. If a drawer has much less front to back than its width, it may tend to swing on the skew sometimes, making it difficult to move. The following instructions are for putting a drawer in one end of the first table (FIG. 6-5C), and it is assumed it will be about halfway along the table. The same method can be used in making any other table with a drawer in the end. Drawers can be placed in both ends, almost meeting in the middle.

25. Mark out legs and rails for two long sides and one end as described, but the drawer end is arranged differently.

26. There are rails above and below the drawer (FIG. 6-10A and B), with the under edge of the lower rail level with the lower edges of the side rails.

27. Allow for the outer edges of the rails to set back from the outer surfaces of the legs the same amount as the side rails. Have their inner edges level with the legs. Groove the top rail for buttons.

28. Cut dovetail joints at the ends of the top rail (FIG. 6-10C and D). Cut double tenons at the ends of the lower rail (FIG. 6-10E and F).

29. Assemble the pair of long sides. The inner surfaces of the rails have to be thickened to form drawer guides for about 2 inches farther than the drawer will enter. Make up the thickness level with the edges of the legs (FIG. 6-10G). A single depth of wood, or two pieces as shown, can be used.

30. Put strips at the top and bottom to form drawer guides. Make their edges level with where the end rails will come. The drawer will slide on the bot-

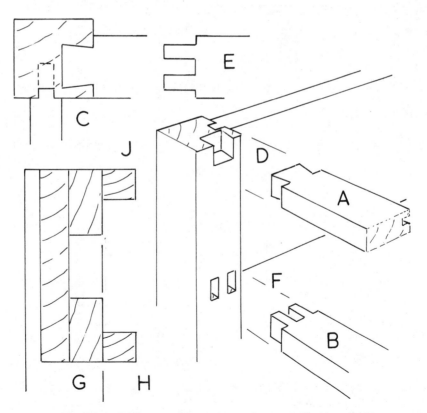

Fig. 6-10. Rail connections when a drawer is fitted to a table.

tom runner (FIG. 6-10H) and is prevented from tilting by the top kicker (FIG. 6-10J). These pieces should be wider than the sides of the drawer.

31. Assemble the framework with the crosswise parts and join to the the top. Exact squareness in all directions is important for the drawer to slide smoothly.

32. Make the drawer fit inside the space in the table, with only enough clearance to allow for movement. Any of the methods described for making drawers in other projects can be used for this, but the following instructions show how to make a dovetailed drawer by traditional methods. It helps to have the table inverted so you can see to test parts in position.

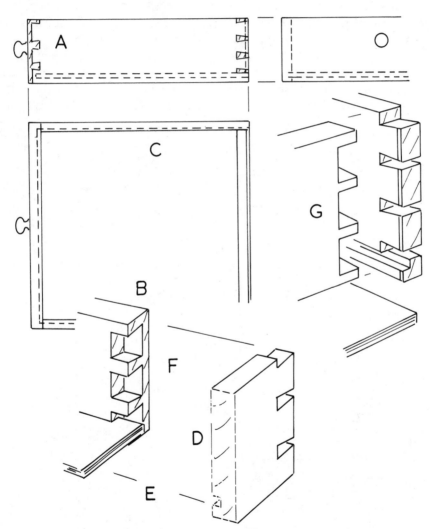

Fig. 6-11. Details of a drawer made in the traditional dovetailed way.

33. Cut the wood for the front (FIG. 6-11A and B) to match the opening in the table. Cut a pair of sides, slightly too long and to a depth to slide between the guides (FIG. 6-11C and D).

34. The bottom of the drawer can be made from solid wood or 1/4-inch plywood. Cut grooves in these three parts to take the bottom (FIG. 6-11E).

35. Cut half-blind dovetail joints between these parts (FIG. 6-11F), so the joint does not show at the front. The bottom groove is hidden in the bottom tail.

36. Fit the drawer back above the groove (FIG. 6-11G) and join it with through dovetails. The tails may extend about 1/16 inch behind the back. The overall width of the drawer back should suit the width between its guides, which should be parallel. For ease of movement you may need to make the drawer marginally narrower at the back than the front.

37. Drill the front for a dowel or screw on the back of a knob.

38. Assemble the drawer parts. Slide in the bottom from the back to hold the other parts square while the glue sets. Plane joints level. Try the assembly in place. When you are satisfied, put the bottom in place, without glue, and screw it upwards under the drawer back. Glue in the knob.

39. Put a block at each side between the drawer guides on the table to stop the drawer when it is pushed in, so the front comes level with the rails.

Railed Table

If a table will have rails between the legs at the top, so you can sit with your legs underneath without obstruction, the rails must be fairly deep to ensure rigidity. If the table will not be used that way, fit lower rails and make the top rails shallower. Several arrangements of lower rails may be seen on earlier furniture, but this example (FIG. 6-12) has two rails between the end legs in the short direction and one long rail between them (FIG. 6-13A). The top rails go all around in the usual way (FIG. 6-13B).

This table is made of fairly light sections of wood, and softwood should not be used. The table looks good if an attractive hardwood is used and given a clear finish. The legs may be left square, or you can turn them between the jointed parts. The suggested sizes (FIG. 6-13C) are for a side table. If you want to vary the size, that need not affect construction.

Materials List
for Railed Table

4 legs	$1^3/4 \times$	$1^3/4$	$\times 29$
2 top rails	$7/8 \times$	3	$\times 32$
2 top rails	$7/8 \times$	3	$\times 16$
2 bottom rails	$7/8 \times$	$1^1/2$	$\times 16$
1 bottom rail	$7/8 \times$	$1^1/2$	$\times 32$
1 top	$7/8 \times$	18	$\times 36$
Button from	$3/4 \times$	$1^1/2$	$\times 30$

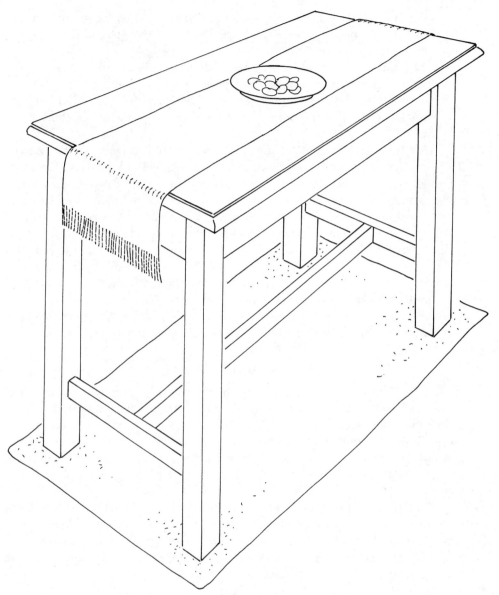

Fig. 6-12. This table has its legs stiffened with lower rails.

1. Mark out the four legs (FIG. 6-14A). A turned pattern is suggested, leaving the areas of the joints square (FIG. 6-14B). You may wish to use your own turned design. Mark out joint details and the limit of the square parts before turning. Leave a little extra at the top of each leg, whether turned or not, which will be trimmed off during assembly.
2. The top rails might b dowelled to the legs, in the way suggested in the previous project, but it is better to use mortise and tenon joints (FIG. 6-14C).

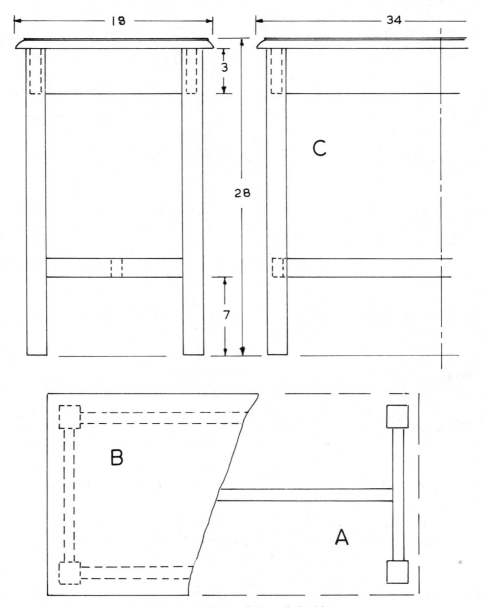

Fig. 6-13. *Sizes of the railed table.*

All tenons in this table may be $1/2$ inch thick. Mark and cut the joints so the tenons penetrate 1 inch (FIG. 6-14D). Miter the meeting ends of the tenons (FIG. 6-14E). Groove the inner surfaces of the top rails for buttons, as in the previous project.

3. The mortise and tenon joints for the legs and the lower rails are straight-forward because each tenon does not have to meet another (FIG. 6-14F).

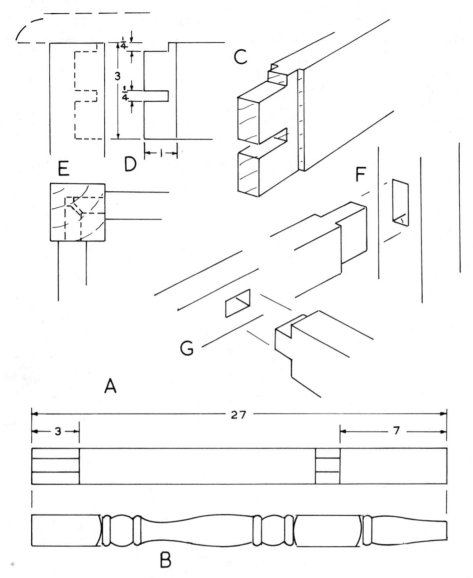

Fig. 6-14. Joints and alternative legs for the railed table.

4. The tenons on the long rail into the short rails are cut across and do not go right through (FIG. 6-14G). Take each tenon as deep as possible, without risking breaking through.
5. Prepare the parts for assembly. Join the legs with the short rails first. Check squareness, lack of twist, and that one end matches the other.
6. When the glue is set, add the lengthways rails. If you think it necessary, you can reinforce the rail-to-rail joints with screws upwards across the

tenons from below the short rails. See that the assembly stands upright on a flat surface. Level the tops of the legs with the rails.

7. Join boards to make up the width of the top. Make it overhang 1 inch or more all around. The edges can be left square, rounded or molded.
8. Prepare ten buttons and attach the top with them in the way described in the last project.
9. Level by trimming the bottom of a leg, if necessary. Take sharpness off the bottoms of legs to avoid marking floor covering. Apply stain and polish.

Storage Cabinet

Early settlers made use of a dry sink, where a bowl and pitcher took the place of our convenient piped water, and buckets and other related equipment were kept on shelves or behind doors. Jelly cupboards were also used as food storage. Both of these pieces of furniture are simple, and some are even primitive, but they provide ideas for reproducing a storage cabinet that has many uses in a modern home, either in the kitchen as a utility item or in a living room as a display piece. Similar cabinets or cupboards have uses in a greenhouse or workshop. One can be used to display and store such things as barbecue equipment on a patio or deck.

This storage cabinet (FIG. 6-15) is similar in general form to some early dry sink and jelly cupboards. The joints are mostly simple and, although some parts are large, not much work needs to be done to them, if you start with prepared boards.

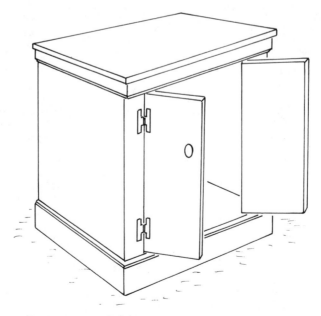

Fig. 6-15. A storage cabinet with a top at table height.

Nearly all the wood is ³/₄ inch thick. You will have to join boards to make up some widths (FIG. 6-16A). Sides can be joined 9-inch boards. Three narrower boards can form the top. If possible, stagger the joints between boards in the sides and the top, so they are not in line with each other when the cabinet is

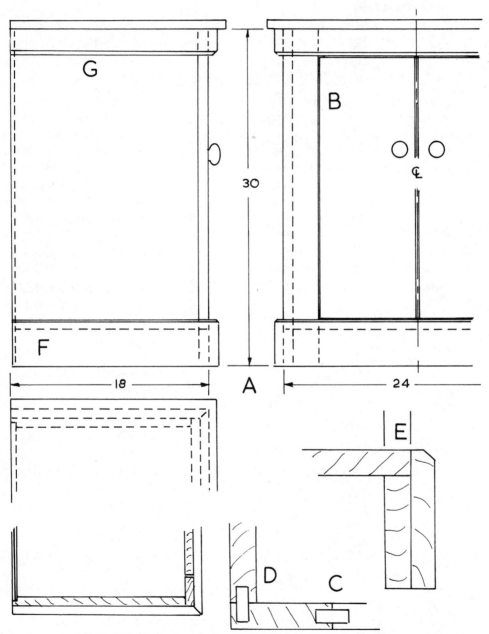

Fig. 6-16. Sizes and sections of the storage cabinet.

assembled. Early cabinets might have been nailed throughout, so you might regard nail heads on exposed surfaces as authentic decorative features. If you wish to avoid nail or screw heads outside, use dowels. Many parts can be screwed from inside, where the heads will not show. Use glue in all joints, although original dry sinks or jelly cupboards depended only on nails.

**Materials List
for Storage Cabinet**

2 sides	$3/4 \times 18$	$\times 32$
2 fronts	$3/4 \times 3$	$\times 32$
2 fronts	$3/4 \times 3$	$\times 20$
2 backs	$3/4 \times 3$	$\times 24$
1 bottom	$3/4 \times 18$	$\times 24$
2 top strips	$3/4 \times$	$3/4 \times 20$
1 plinth	$3/4 \times$	$33/4 \times 28$
2 plinths	$3/4 \times$	$33/4 \times 21$
1 molding	$3/4 \times 3$	$\times 28$
2 moldings	$3/4 \times 3$	$\times 21$
2 doors	$3/4 \times 9$	$\times 26$
1 top	$3/4 \times 20$	$\times 29$
1 back	$1/4 \times 24$	$\times 31$ plywood

1. Prepare sufficient wood for all parts, including gluing where necessary to make up widths.
2. Make the front frame. This has 3-inch sides the full height of the cabinet (FIGS. 6-16B and 17A), with pieces across (FIG. 6-17B) to make up the cabinet's width. Join these parts with two $3/8$-inch dowels in each joint (FIG. 6-16C). Check squareness by comparing diagonal measurements.
3. Make the two sides (FIG. 6-17C). Rabbet the rear edges for the plywood back. Prepare the front edges and frame for dowels to supplement glue (FIGS. 6-16D and 17D). Five dowels should be sufficient.
4. Make strips to go between the top and bottom edges of the sides inside the rabbets (FIG. 6-17E). The bottom strip should be the same height as the crosspiece of the front frame. Prepare the ends of the strips and the cabinet sides for the dowels.
5. Join together all the parts made so far. See that the assembly is square when viewed from above, and that it stands firmly on a level surface.
6. Put strips across the inside, level with the front and rear pieces (FIG. 6-17F), to support the bottom.
7. Make the bottom (FIG. 6-17G) notched around the front frame sides with its edge level with the outside of the frame (FIG. 6-16E). Glue and screw, or nail it in place.
8. No shelves are shown. If you want any, place supporting strips across the sides so the shelves can rest on them and be lifted out. Do not make shelves with edges too close to the front, or they may hide articles put below them.

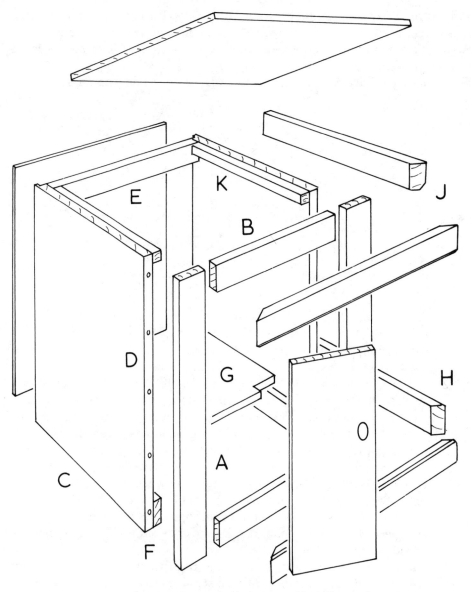

Fig. 6-17. How parts of the storage cabinet fit together.

9. Fit the plywood back with glue and pins into the rabbets and to the cross-pieces.
10. Make plinth strips (FIGS. 6-16F and 17H) to the same height as the cabinet bottom. Bevel the outer edges or mold them. Cut the strips so they are level with the back, and miter them around the front corners. Attach them with glue and screws from inside.

11. Make the top molding in the same way (FIGS. 6-16G and 17J), with the lower edges in line with the top part of the front frame.
12. Put strips across inside the top edges of the sides (FIG. 6-17K) for screws upwards into the top.
13. Make the top level at the back, but overhang 3/4 inch at sides and front. In an original cupboard, the edges were left square. You can round, bevel or mold them.
14. Attach the top with screws upwards through the side strips. If necessary, deeply counterbore the front and rear strips and drill screws through them.
15. The doors are two boards. If possible, obtain quarter-sawn boards (with the end-grain lines across the thickness of a board) to avoid any risk of warping. Otherwise, battens can be placed across the inside of each door, a few inches from top and bottom, screwed from inside to resist movement in the doors.
16. Cut the doors to fit easily in the front frame with enough clearance between them.
17. You can let in hinges, but early cabinets had surface hinges, either of the H pattern or with decorative outlines. Round wood knobs are appropriate for this cabinet. Put a small piece of wood so it projects below the top frame to act as a stop for the doors. Although not authentic for a reproduction, ball catches let into the bottom edges of the doors are the most convenient fasteners for these doors.
18. Early cabinets were left untreated and scrubbed occasionally or painted. You can use paint or treat the wood with a sealer or varnish to fill the grain and give an untreated appearance without risking that dirt will enter the wood.

Small Cabinet

This cabinet (FIG. 6-18) stands a little higher than a table. It has a cupboard and two shelves that can hold books, ornaments or other small items. There are handles so the whole unit can be lifted, and it does not have to remain in one place, but can be moved next to a chair or elsewhere that its contents are required. The sizes as drawn (FIG. 6-19) suit this intended use, but you can make it bigger.

The cabinet is best made of a good quality hardwood so it matches other furniture, although it is possible to make it of softwood and give it a painted finish. Most parts are 3/4 inch thick. Construction described is by traditional methods, with dado and mortise and tenon joints, so your final piece of furniture is a reasonably authentic reproduction. You can use dowels for some joints. The door panel is solid wood, prepared in the traditional way, but the cupboard back, which would have been solid, can be made of plywood, since it normally is not visible and that is more convenient.

Most of the work is in the pair of sides. Then the crosswise parts are made and the door is fitted after these pieces are assembled.

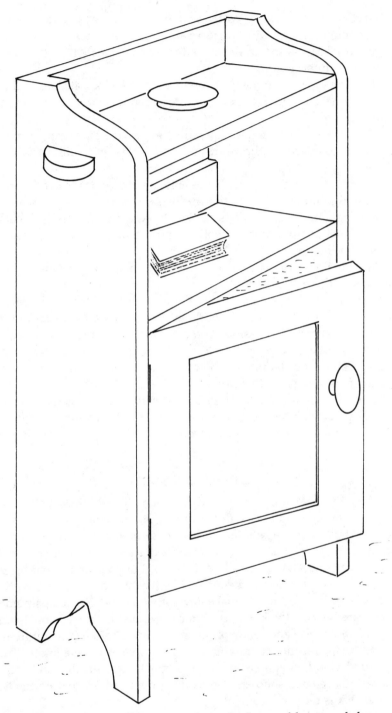

Fig. 6-18. This small cabinet stands on the floor and has two shelves.

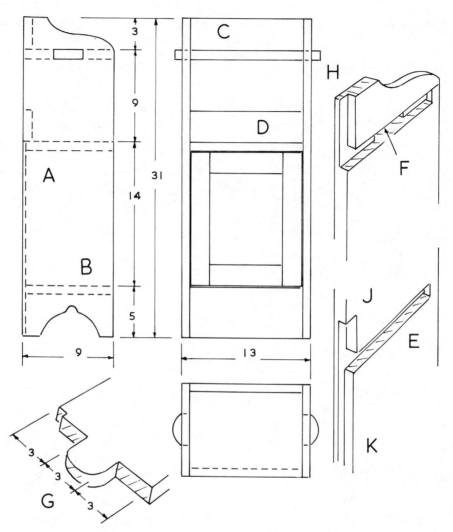

Fig. 6-19. Sizes and joints of the small cabinet.

**Materials List
for Small Cabinet**

2 sides	3/4 ×	9 × 33
2 shelves	3/4 ×	9 × 15
1 shelf	3/4 ×	9 × 17
2 backs	3/4 ×	3 × 15
2 door frames	1 ×	2 × 15
2 door frames	1 ×	2 × 13
1 door panel	1/2 ×	9 × 13
1 back	1/4 ×	13 × 24 plywood

1. Mark out the pair of sides (FIG. 6-19A) with the positions of the other parts on the inner surfaces. Draw the shaped top (FIG. 6-20A) and the bottom (FIG. 6-20B) on both sides. Do not cut anything at this stage.

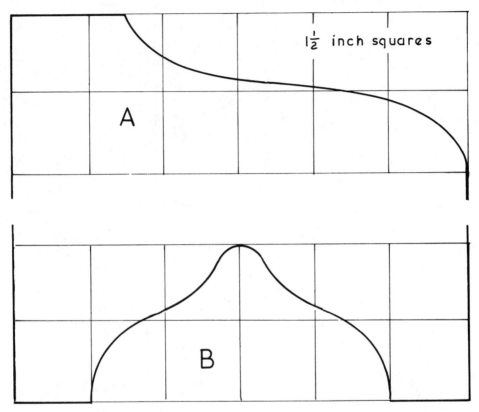

Fig. 6-20. Shaped parts of the small cabinet.

2. Prepare the two lower shelves (FIG. 6-19B) and the two backs (FIG. 6-19C and D), all to the same length.
3. The shelves fit into the sides with stopped dado joints. Cut grooves for the shelves to within 3/8 inch of the front edges (FIG. 6-19E).
4. At the upper grooves, cut through centrally 3 inches wide so the shelf ends project as handles (FIG. 6-19F). Make the top shelf the same length between shoulders as the other shelves, but the tenons should go through and project (FIG. 6-19G).
5. Prepare the rear edges of the sides to take the back parts. Cut away at the top for the upper back, with a recess the same depth as the groove (FIG. 6-19H). Cut at the middle shelf for the other back in the same way (FIG. 6-19J). Cut a rabbet behind the middle shelf and down to the floor level in both sides to take the plywood back (FIG. 6-19K).

6. Round the extending tenons on the top shelf to make comfortable grips. Cut the tops and bottoms of the sides.

7. Glue the shelves into their grooves. Glue both backs into their recesses and to the shelves. Thin screws can also be used at the ends of the backs into the sides and upwards through the shelves. Fit the plywood back, with glue and pins. Stop it within 1/4 inch of the floor, so it does not interfere with the corner feet.

8. The plywood should hold the assembly square, but check squareness, particularly at the door opening.

9. The door fits in the traditional way, inside the shelves and sides, with its front surfaces level with them. Use grooved frames joined with mortise and tenon joints. The panel is 1/2-inch wood, thinned around the edges to fit the grooves.

10. Prepare sufficient wood with grooves 1/4 inch wide (FIG. 6-21A).

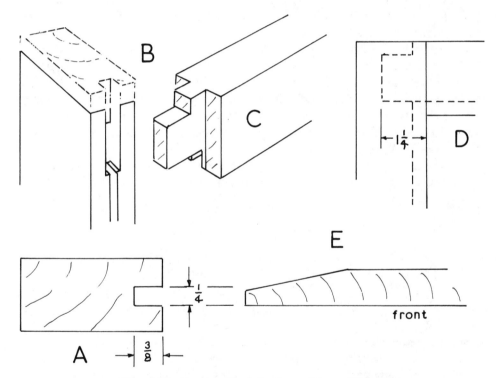

Fig. 6-21. Construction of a door with a solid panel.

11. Mark the lengths of the sides from the door opening, allowing 1/8 inch for clearance. Cut the wood about 1/4 inch beyond the marked end (FIG. 6-21B). Leave this on until the door is assembled. The extra wood resists breaking out when the joints are cut and allows you to trim the assembled door more accurately to size.

12. Mark the top and bottom of the door with lines at what will be the shoulders of the joints, so the finished door has a 1/8-inch clearance in the width.
13. Mark the tenons (FIG. 6-21C and D). Make the tenons one-third of the thickness of the wood, if possible, but you might need to vary this a little to suit your tools. Cut the tenons.
14. Cut the mortises to match, taking them a little too deep, so the joints will pull tight against the shoulders.
15. With the door frame parts as guides, prepare the solid panel. Allow for it going 1/4 inch into each groove. Bevel the rear surface (FIG. 6-21E) all around. Pencil the width and thickness required. The panel should make a fairly tight fit when the door is assembled, but because it is not glued it will probably expand and contract a little with varying amounts of moisture in the air. If the cabinet will be used in a centrally heated room and you are making it in a colder shop, it helps to store the panel wood for a few weeks in the conditions it will have to withstand before making the door to stabilize the wood.
16. Assemble the door with glue in the joints, but the panel fitted dry, with its beveled side inwards. When the glue has set, cut off the projecting parts of the sides. Trim the door to make an easy fit in its opening.
17. Let in two, 1 1/2-inch hinges at one side of the door. Make or buy a wood knob about 1 1/2 inch diameter. Put a small stop on the cabinet side, so the door closes flush. Use a ball, spring or magnetic catch to hold the door closed. An original cabinet would have probably had a turnbutton mounted on the edge of the side, but that may be considered ugly today.
18. You will probably choose a furniture finish of stain and polish.

Storage Bench

Early housewives did much of their kitchen work on a table with storage underneath. This was a substantial, if crude, construction and had to stand up to much domestic work as well as food preparation. We might not want a table for that sort of work anymore, but a bench or table with plenty of storage underneath still has uses about the home in other places besides the kitchen. It can be used in the garage or garden shed. It makes a good light bench for your workshop.

Early storage benches were mostly of nailed construction. This bench (FIG. 6-22) can have many parts nailed, although it is neater and stronger to use screws. Some parts might be dowelled or joined with mortises and tenons.

For the sizes shown (FIG. 6-23A) most of the wood can be 1 inch thick. For heavy work in a shop, you may wish to make the top thicker, but this is not intended to take the place of the general-purpose woodworking bench. The top has a good overhang so there is space for clamping on work or fitting light vises

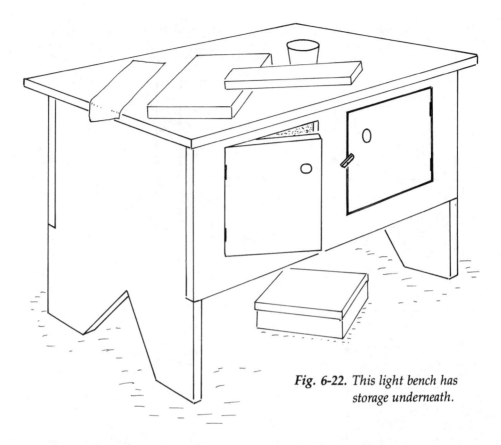

Fig. 6-22. This light bench has storage underneath.

or other equipment with clamp attachments. For many purposes, softwood should be satisfactory, but a hardwood top is better able to withstand rough use.

The ends form legs and are joined with a solid back and front frame with openings for two doors. A bottom fits inside and the top is nailed or screwed on.

**Materials List
for Storage Bench**

2 frames	1	×	3	×	20
1 frame	1	×	3	×	18
2 frames	1	×	3	×	29
2 ends	1	×	18	×	32
1 back	1	×	18	×	29
2 top strips	1	×	3	×	18
2 bottom supports	1	×	2	×	18
2 bottom supports	1	×	2	×	27
1 bottom	1	×	16	×	27
2 doors	1	×	9	×	14
1 top	1	×	22	×	33

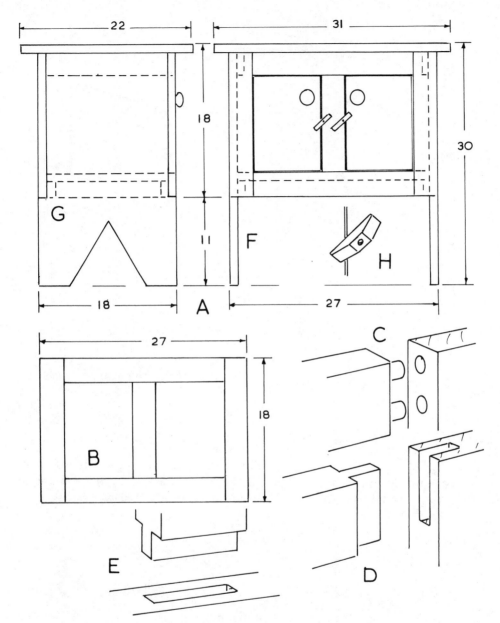

Fig. 6-23. Sizes and details of the storage bench.

1. Make the front frame (FIGS. 6-23B and 24A) first. All parts are 3 inches wide. When the frame is built into the table, it gets strength from other parts, but its pieces should still be joined strongly. You can dowel the corners (FIG. 6-23C). The joints can be mortise and tenon (FIG. 6-23D), and can be open since they will be covered by other parts.

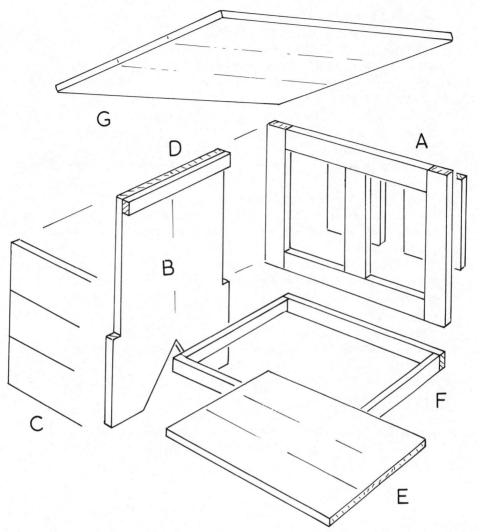

Fig. 6-24. *How parts of the storage bench fit together.*

2. The central upright can also be dowelled, or short tenons can be used (FIG. 6-23E). Assemble the parts squarely.

3. Make the two ends (FIGS. 6-23F and 24B) from boards joined to make the width. Cut recesses at the sides, deep enough for the front frame and the back, which will be the same size. Cut a V at the bottom to form feet.

4. Prepare sufficient boards to make the back (FIG. 6-24C). They can be glued together, although it probably is satisfactory to nail or screw them in place without gluing.

5. Join the frame and the back to the legs to form a squared assembly. In the simplest assembly, you can nail and leave the nail heads exposed. Screws

with their heads left showing can be used. It is neater to counterbore for screws, then glue plugs over the heads.

6. Put strips across inside the tops of the legs (FIG. 6-24D).

7. Make the bottom (FIG. 6-24E) so it fits inside the other parts. You might be able to use unglued boards for some purposes, otherwise glue boards to make up the width.

8. Arrange supports for the bottom with strips around so it is level with the top edge of the bottom strip of the front frame (FIGS. 6-23G and 24F).

9. Nail or screw the strips in place and fasten them to the bottom. This locks the structure in shape and the bench should stand without wobbling on a flat surface.

10. Make the top to overhang 2 inches all around (FIG. 6-24G). Use counterbored screws to fasten it. For most purposes, the top can be made from boards glued together, but for some work fastening the boards without gluing may be sufficient.

11. The doors are best made from quartersawn wood (see instructions for the storage cabinet). Put strips across inside to stiffen the doors, if you think it necessary. The doors should have a little clearance in their openings. You can let in 2-inch hinges between the doors and their posts, or use decorative surface hinges. Turned knobs are appropriate handles. Turnbuttons on the central upright (FIG. 6-23H) are traditional fasteners but spring or magnetic catches can be used. If the catches do not also act as stops, put wood behind the top corners of the door openings to prevent the doors swinging too far inwards.

12. The finish will depend on the wood and the intended use. For some purposes, the storage bench can be untreated. A light color paint inside helps you to see things in the quite commodious interior.

7

Utility items

Several things made from wood do not fall into particular categories of furniture, but are just as useful and often as decorative now as they were to early makers and users. Most are small and portable and are intended to serve particular purposes. In some cases there is no need for the original purpose. Such a piece of furniture is not just a curio, however, but can have modern applications. Some can be regarded as accessories to other furniture or life in the home, but all are primarily useful so they are grouped here as utility items.

Carrier/Magazine Rack

This carrier for needlework and other household work can also be a rack for newspapers (FIG. 7-1). All the parts are linked with mortise and tenon joints, using glue and no nails or screws.

To keep the carrier light, make it from a close-grained hardwood no more than 1/2 inch finished thickness. If a coarser hardwood is used, increase the thicknesses to 9/16 inch. If you choose softwood, it is better to use 5/8-inch thickness throughout. If following tradition is not important, you can use 1/2-inch plywood for all the parts, preferably a hardwood type. Sizes suggested (FIG. 7-2A) should make a rack large enough for most magazines or give ample room for needlework, knitting or other chairside requirements.

There are two ends cut with mortises and six lengthwise parts that tenon into them. Use well-seasoned wood to reduce the risk of warping. If you have doubts about seasoning, keep the wood for a few weeks in the atmosphere where the carrier will be used. If you select wood with the end-grain lines going across the thickness of the wood, that is least likely to warp and is preferred for the ends.

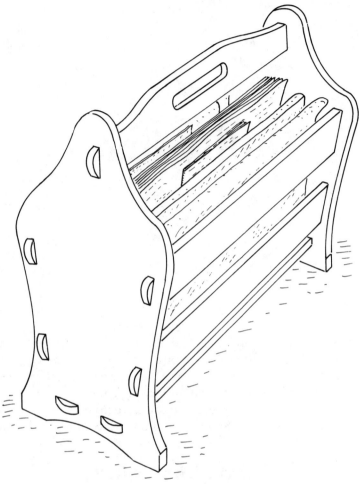

Fig. 7-1. *This carrier can be used for magazines or other things.*

**Materials List for
Carrier/Magazine
Rack**

(All ¹/₂ inch to ⁵/₈
inch thick—
see instructions)

2 ends	10 × 17
4 rails	3 × 18
1 bottom	6 × 18
1 handle	3 × 18

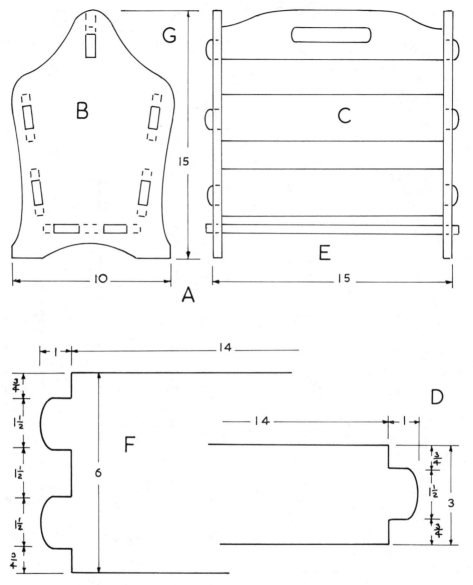

Fig. 7-2. Sizes of the carrier/magazine rack.

1. Mark out the pair of ends (FIG. 7-2B), working about a centerline (FIG. 7-3A). All mortises are 1¹/2 inch long, but mark the width to suit the actual thickness of wood that will fit into them. A good fit helps in assembly and final rigidity. Do not cut the outline yet and leave the mortises until you can match them to the tenons.

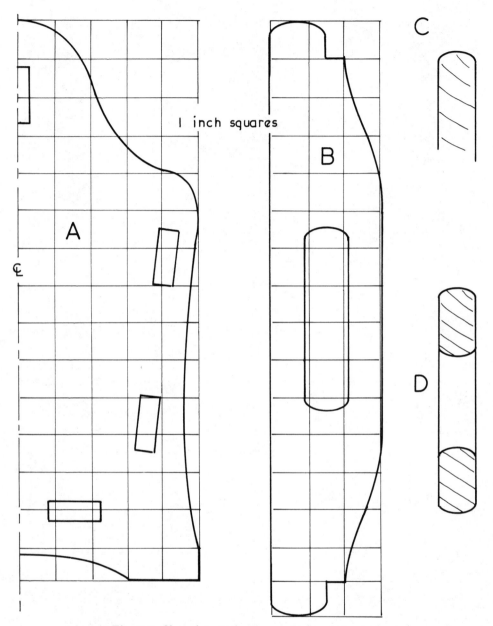

I inch squares

A

B

C

D

℄

Fig. 7-3. *Shaped parts for the carrier/magazine rack.*

2. Make the four side rails (FIG. 7-2C). Make sure they are the same length between the shoulders. The tenons will project through the ends 1/2 inch, and should be rounded (FIG. 7-2D).

3. Make the bottom (FIG. 7-2E) the same length as the side rails and with double tenons (FIG. 7-2F). Treat the tenon ends the same way.

4. Cut the handle (FIG. 7-2G) the same length as the other parts, with tenons

the same size (FIG. 7-3B). Cut the hand hole by drilling the ends and removing the waste. Shape the top edge.

5. Compare the tenons on lengthwise parts with the marked mortises they will have to fit, and cut the mortises. Mark the matched parts.

6. When you are satisfied with the joints, cut the outlines of the ends.

7. You can leave the edges square and just take sharpness off the angles, but the whole rack looks better if all the exposed edges are rounded. An elliptical section (FIG. 7-3C) looks better than a semi-circular one. Do the same on the ends of the tenons. Round the edges of the hand hole (FIG. 7-3D).

8. Sand all parts, then assemble the lengthwise pieces to one end and add the other end. The assembly should pull square, but try standing it on a level surface to check for twist before the glue sets.

9. Finish a hardwood piece with stain and polish. Softwood can be painted. If you used plywood, seal the edges before painting.

Drying Frame

This drying frame or towel rack (FIG. 7-4) is intended for a counter top or table and serves as a towel rack or for drying smaller cloths in a kitchen or laundry room. The two frames can be moved separately or brought together when out of use, and are arranged to tilt each way so things hanging from the rails are clear of each other. The base is heavy enough so the frame is steady and it has a lip so it can become a tray for oddments or folded cloths.

The sizes (FIG. 7-5) should suit most purposes, but measure where you intend to use the rack and modify some dimensions if necessary.

Parts can be made of hardwood or softwood, or they can be mixed, with the frame softwood and the base parts hardwood to provide a stabilizing weight.

Materials List for Drying Frame

2 ends	3/4 ×	21/2 ×	14
4 ends	3/4 ×	21/2 ×	6
1 base	1 ×	12 ×	28
2 lips	3/8 ×	21/2 ×	28
2 frame sides	3/4 ×	11/2 ×	28
4 rails	3/4 ×	11/2 ×	24

1. The key parts that control some of the other measurements are the pair of ends (FIG. 7-5B). They are two thicknesses, with pieces across joined by matching pieces that act as stops. The angle of slope when the frames are opened is 20° each side of vertical.

2. Cut the two outside ends (FIG. 7-6A), then make the stop pieces to the angle (FIG. 7-6B) and glue them together. True the curved outlines to match each other. Drill for 1/2-inch dowels (FIG. 7-7A).

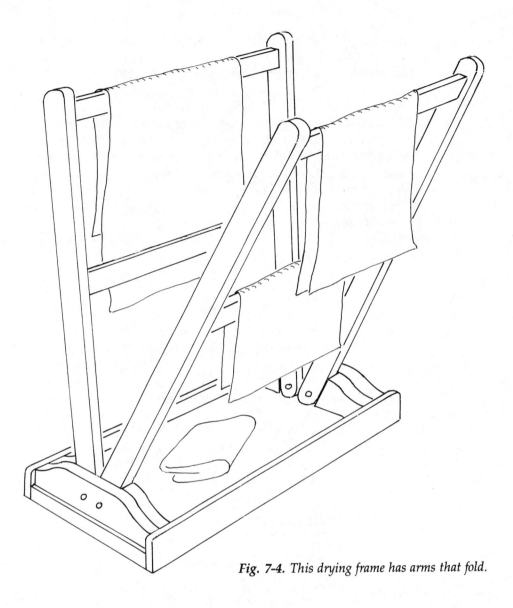

Fig. 7-4. This drying frame has arms that fold.

3. Mark out the four frame sides (FIGS. 7-5C, 6C and 7B). Curve the bottoms with the dowel hole as center. For strength at the top, extend the curved end $1^{1}/4$ inch above the mortise. Mark the mortise positions, but delay cutting them until the matching tenons are ready.

4. Make the four rails (FIGS. 7-6D and 7C). Cut the tenons $1/2$ inch thick (FIG. 7-6E) and round the edges.

5. Assemble the frames squarely and check that they match each other. It is sufficient to glue the mortise and tenon joints, but you can wedge the tenons for extra strength.

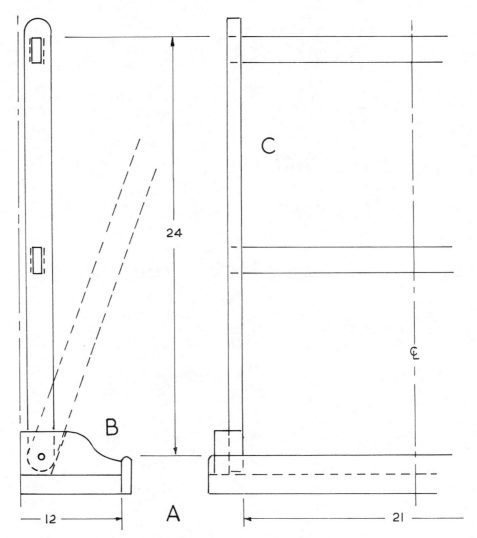

Fig. 7-5. Sizes of the drying frame.

6. Use the frames as guides for spacing the ends when you mark out the base. The width of the base should match the ends (FIG. 7-6F), but project 1/4 inch past them.

7. Glue the ends to the base. Use screws from below for extra strength.

8. Add lips each side (FIGS. 7-6G and 7D). Round the upper edge of each lip and round its ends down to the base.

9. The dowels that form pivots do not need to be glued. If they are loose you can knock them out if you ever need to take the frame apart.

10. The bottom can be stained or painted and the frames left untreated, or just sealed with varnish.

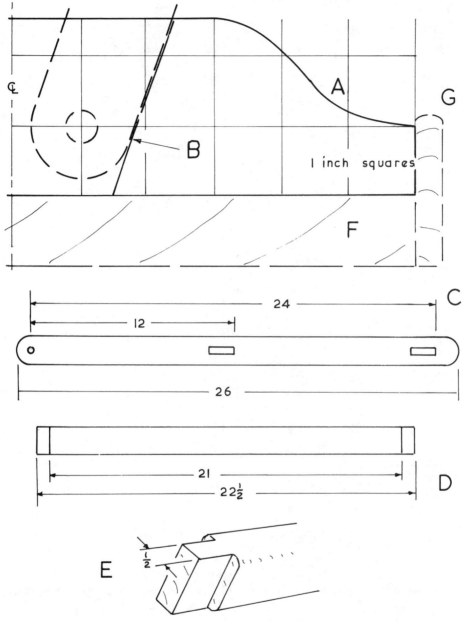

C̵

B

A

G

1 inch squares

F

24

12

26

C

21

22½

D

E

½

Fig. 7-6. *Parts of the drying frame.*

Steps

These steps (FIG. 7-8) allow you to step up on two, 8-inch stages, enabling you to reach most shelves and cabinets in the home. The steps are rigid, but light enough to lift about. They avoid the weakness and possible danger of folding

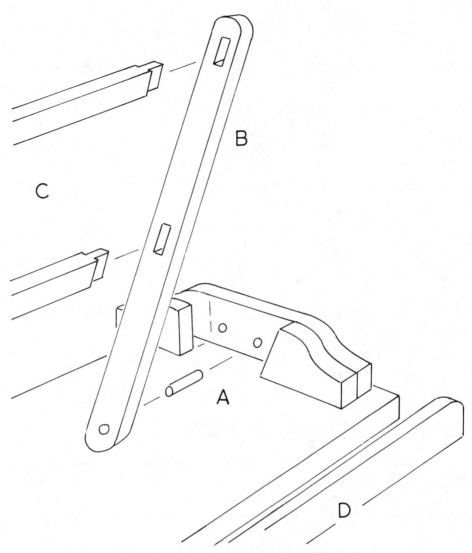

Fig. 7-7. How parts of the drying frame fit together.

steps. The top step is also a height suitable for sitting, giving the piece a second-ary use as a stool.

All the parts can be softwood finished with paint, or a hardwood can be used if the stool is to become part of the furnishing of a living room or den. The joints suggested give an assembly that should stand up to fairly rough usage.

If the sizes are altered, see that the rise is the same from floor to first step and from that to the top step. Let the rear edge of the lower step come under the center of the top step. For stability, see that the legs project a few inches behind the line of the rear of the top step.

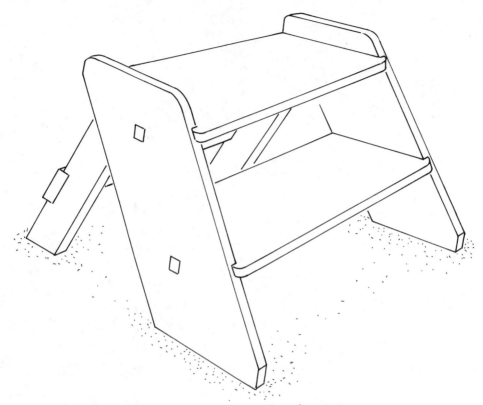

Fig. 7-8. These steps are rigid and stable.

Join the steps to the sides with dado joints, with stiffeners underneath (FIG. 7-9A) and tenons through the sides. The legs are glued and screwed inside the sides and are joined by a rail (FIG. 7-9B). It might be helpful to set out the main lines of a side view to get the angles, but these can also be obtained from FIG. 7-11.

Materials List for Steps

2 sides	$7/8 \times 6 \times 22$
2 steps	$7/8 \times 7 \times 18$
2 stiffeners	$1 \times 2 \times 18$
2 rear legs	$7/8 \times 2 \times 18$
1 rear rail	$1 \times 2 \times 18$

1. Mark out the pair of sides (FIGS. 7-9C, 10A and 11A). See that all lines for steps and ends are at the same angle. The stiffeners are at the centers of the steps.
2. Cut the dado grooves (FIG. 7-10B) to suit the thickness of wood that will be used for the steps.

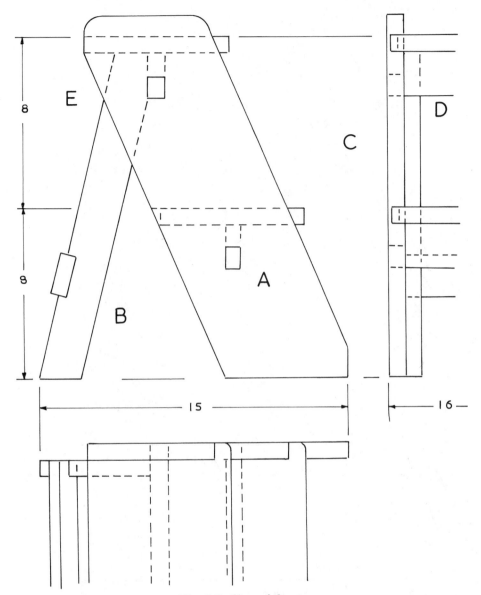

Fig. 7-9. Sizes of the steps.

3. Cut the two steps the same size (FIG. 7-10C and D). Trim the ends to fit around the sides at the front and around the projecting corners.
4. Make the two stiffeners (FIGS. 7-9D and 10E).
5. Cut tenons on the ends and matching mortises in the legs (FIG. 7-10E).
6. Cut the ends of the sides to shape. Round the upper edges and corners. Round the edges of the steps and the lower edges of the stiffeners.

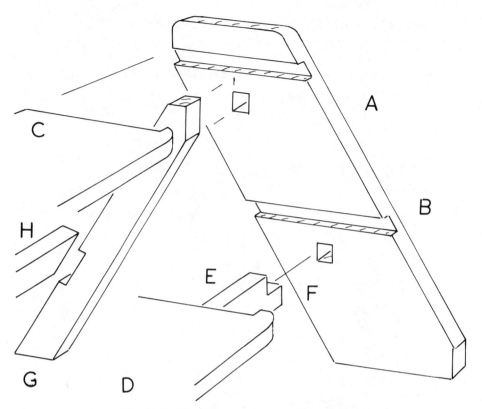

Fig. 7-10. How parts of the steps fit together.

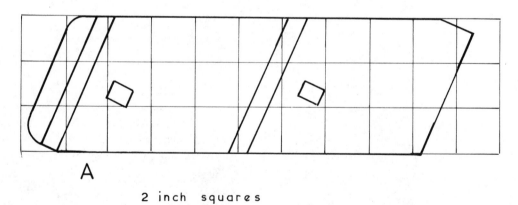

A

2 inch squares

B

Fig. 7-11. Shapes of parts of the steps.

7. Assemble the parts. Glue the stiffeners under the steps. You can drive a few nails or screws downwards through the steps. It should be sufficient to glue the tenons in their mortises, but the tenons can be wedged for extra strength. Glue the steps in their grooves and drive three screws into each joint from outside, although if you do not want screw heads showing outside they could be driven diagonally upwards from inside. The parts should pull each other square, but check squareness by comparing diagonal measurements before the glue sets.

8. Make the two rear legs (FIGS. 7-10G and 11B). Cut the tops of the legs so they fit closely behind the stiffeners (FIG. 7-9E). Check that when a leg is in position its bottom cut follows in line with the bottom of the assembled side.

9. Cut notches in the rear legs, allowing a rail to fit in for half its thickness (FIG. 7-10H).

10. Glue and screw the rear legs inside the step sides. Make the rear rail a little too long. Glue and screw it in the leg notches, then trim the ends level.

11. Check that the steps will stand without wobbling on a flat surface. If necessary, level the bottoms by trimming the end of one or more feet. Bevel around the bottoms to reduce risk of splintering. See that all sharp and rough edges are removed, then apply your chosen finish.

Rotating Desk Tidy

One way early settlers kept letters and important papers was in notches sawn in the edge of a piece of wood. A series of diagonal cuts allowed papers to be stored safely and compactly. This desk tidy uses the same idea and develops it to make a stand for pens, pencils and many smaller items. If an early craftsman made one of these stands he would mount it on a peg to allow rotation. He did not have the availability of 'Lazy Susan' bearings to help him. It is suggested you use one of them, but the alternative peg mounting is shown as well.

The rotating desk tidy (FIG. 7-12) is built around a solid block, cut to make the letter rack, which can be used for envelopes, postcards and similar papers as well as correspondence. Below that is a tray with a block of four holes for pencils or pens. All of this is supported over a base the same size as the tray, so you can turn the tidy any way you wish.

Materials List for Rotating Desk Tidy

1 block	2	× 4	× 9
1 block	2	× 2	× 3
1 base	1/2	× 7	× 7
1 tray bottom	1/2	× 6	× 6
4 tray frames	3/8	× 11/4	× 8

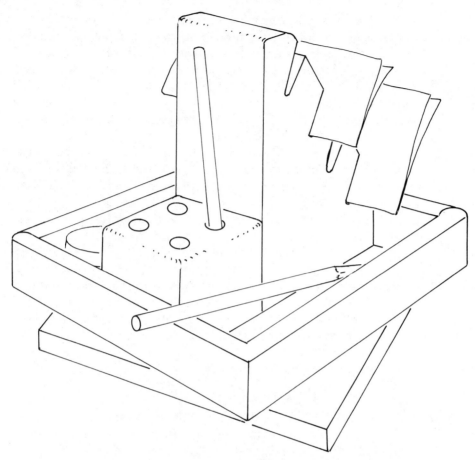

Fig. 7-12. This desk tidy revolves and has sections for papers and pens.

1. Start with the main block (FIG. 7-13A), which is cut from 2-inch by 4-inch wood sections. Square and taper the ends (FIG. 7-14A).
2. Drill $3/16$-inch-diameter holes at what will be the bottom of the letter slots (FIG. 7-14B). Mark the tapers of the slots and cut carefully into the holes. Sand inside the slots with abrasive paper wrapped around a steel rule, or something similar.
3. Make a 2-inch cube block that will hold pens and pencils (FIG. 7-13B). Check the sizes of your pens and pencils. Drill holes that will take them easily—probably between $3/8$ inch and $1/2$ inch diameter (FIG. 7-14C). Drill through the block, as the tray bottom will act as a stop.
4. Round all edges and corners that will be exposed on these two blocks. Glue them together.
5. Make a tray bottom that forms a 6-inch square under the joined blocks (FIG. 7-13C). Glue and screw it to the blocks with two edges level with the blocks and an equal projection on each side.

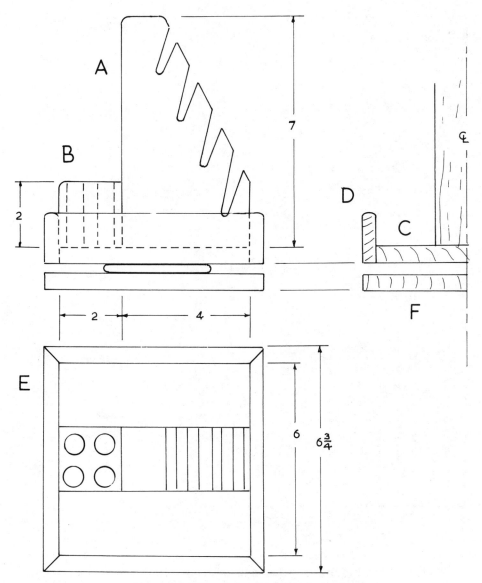

Fig. 7-13. Sizes of the revolving desk tidy.

6. Prepare sufficient strips with rounded top edges to make a frame around the tray (FIG. 7-13D). Cut pieces with mitered corners to fit and join this frame to the tray bottom (FIG. 7-13E) with glue and fine pins, that can be punched below the surface and covered with stopping.

7. Make a base (FIGS. 7-13F and 14D) the same size as the complete tray.

8. If you are using a "Lazy Susan" bearing, it can be 3 inches in diameter. Fit it temporarily between the parts, then remove it to finish the wood.

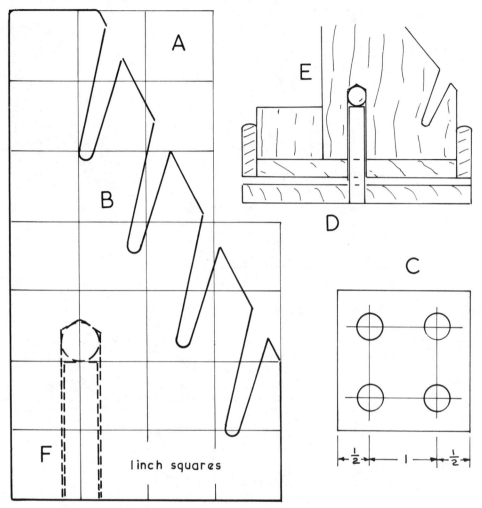

Fig. 7-14. Parts of the desk tidy.

9. For a peg mounting, the hole must be drilled squarely and be a moving fit over the peg, but do not make it so slack that it will wobble. Drill the hole about 2 inches deep (FIG. 7-14E and F).

10. Use a glass or metal ball in the hole as a bearing. This should be no larger than the diameter of the rod. Fit a rod at the center of the base and cut its length so there is no more than $1/8$-inch clearance between the tray and the base.

11. Finish the tidy to suit the wood. It can be painted brightly all over, or it can be stained and polished. If cloth is glued under the base it will prevent slipping or marking a polished surface. Strips of cloth can be placed inside the tray.

Kitchen Boards

An expert cook or chef always prefers to work on wood. Despite the coming of plastics into all aspects of modern life, there is still a preference in the kitchen for wood on which to cut meat and vegetables and roll pastry.

A board has often been a single piece of wood, which is sometimes satisfactory. But besides its tendency to warp, a single piece of wood presents a surface that may wear unevenly. Such a board can be stiffened against warping by placing strips across underneath, but they make the board one-sided, and it is convenient to be able to turn a board over and use opposite sides for different operations. It is better to use the butcherblock technique and build up the board with a large number of strips glued edge-to-edge. There is less likely to be differences in texture and the varying grain arrangements in the many pieces help each other to resist warping or other movement. This laminated construction should ensure the board remains flat. The effect is pleasing and such boards have a professional appearance. Boards can also serve as kitchen hot pads. A pan of boiling food or a dish from the oven should not sit directly on the countertop. Solid boards can be used, but it is better to have pads with air spaces that carry away some of the heat.

The boards described first are for pastry rolling, chopping and cutting (FIG. 7-15). Hot pads follow. The wood should be a clean type, free from resin, oil or

Fig. 7-15. *A variety of boards are needed in a kitchen.*

odor. Ideally, it is a close-grained hardwood of light color. Although color does not have any effect, pale color looks hygienic. If most things in the kitchen are a light color, you may want dark boards. Widths of individual pieces do not matter, and you may make a board with strips of different widths. Pieces should not be too wide, or the butcherblock effect will be lost and there can be a risk of a wide strip warping. For a large board, do not exceed 3 inches, and for this and smaller boards it is better for strips to be no more than half this width. Use a waterproof glue, preferably a boatbuilding type, but avoid resorcinol, with its dark color. A modern glue clamped properly has adequate strength and there is no need for dowels between strips.

**Materials List for
Kitchen Boards**

(Typical sections, but
you can use others)

Cutting board

| 5 pieces | $5/8$ $\times$ $11/2$ $\times$ 9 |

Chopping board

| 6 pieces | 1 $\times$ $11/2$ $\times$ 10 |
| 1 handle | $11/4$ $\times$ $11/4$ $\times$ 8 |

Pastry board

| 10 pieces | $3/4$ $\times$ $11/2$ $\times$ 19 |
| 1 handle | $1/2$ $\times$ 2 $\times$ 12 |

First hot pad

| 4 pieces | $1/4$ $\times$ $11/4$ $\times$ 8 |
| 2 pieces | $1/2$ $\times$ $3/4$ $\times$ 8 |

Second hot pad

4 pieces	$1/4$ $\times$ $11/4$ $\times$ 8
2 pieces	$1/2$ $\times$ $3/4$ $\times$ 8
4 borders	$1/4$ $\times$ 1 $\times$ 8
or	$1/2$ $\times$ $3/4$ $\times$ 8

Third hot pad

| 8 pieces | $3/4$ $\times$ $3/4$ $\times$ 8 |
| 4 borders | $1/4$ $\times$ $3/4$ $\times$ 8 |

1. To make a cutting board (FIG. 7-16A), prepare sufficient strips. See that edges are square. Unless power planer blades are very sharp and the wood is fed slowly, there is a tendency for the surface to be pounded, so it becomes 'case-hardened' and resistant to glue absorption. This can be cured by taking off a shaving with a hand plane.
2. Cut the strips a little too long at first, for trimming later.
3. You can arrange and glue all the strips in one operation, but it is easier to get the surfaces flat and joints close if you first join them in pairs, then bring the pairs together, until you have made up the width (FIG. 7-16B).

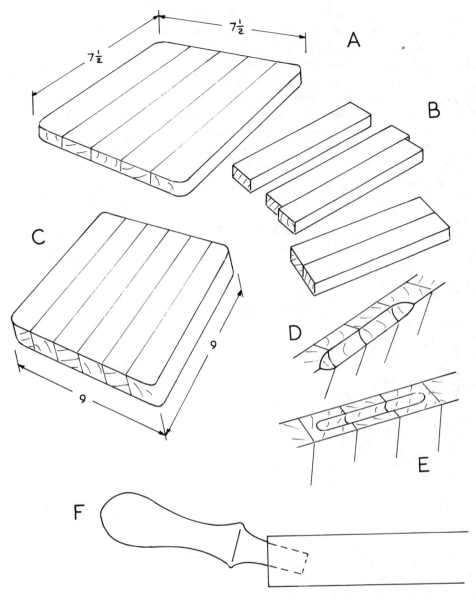

Fig. 7-16. Butcherblock construction of kitchen boards.

4. Scrape off excess glue and plane the surfaces level. Mark out the shape, including rounding corners, then finish the board as if it were a single piece of wood. Round the edges.
5. Sand thoroughly, then wet the wood and allow it to dry. This raises tiny bits of fiber the first sanding bent instead of removing. Sand again lightly to remove them.

6. You can limit water absorption by soaking the wood in a vegetable oil, such as cooking oil. Several treatments over the first few weeks will impregnate the wood sufficiently.
7. A chopping block (FIG. 7-16C) can be made in the same way, but should be thicker. It is heavy, but that is an advantage. You do not want the board moving about as you chop over a table or countertop.
8. You can cut finger notches (FIG. 7-16D) under opposite sides of a chopping block, to make lifting easier. Alternatively, with a suitable router cutter, you can cut hollows in the edges (FIG. 7-16E). One advantage of doing this is you can lift the board when using either side.
9. There can also be a turned handle (FIG. 7-16F). If it is fit straight into an edge, the board can be used either side up, but arranging it at an angle makes lifting it easier.
10. A pastry board (FIG. 7-17A) is made in the same way as the smaller boards. Choose wood without flaws and reasonably straight grain.

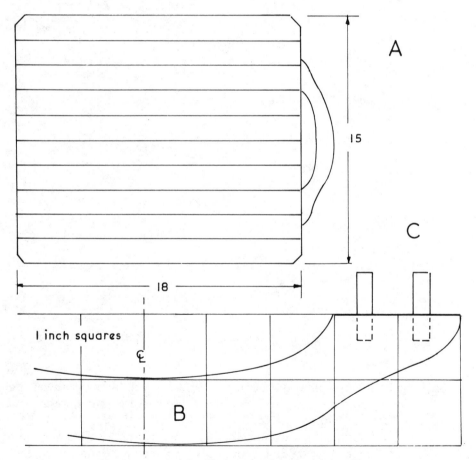

Fig. 7-17. A butcherblock pastry board with handle.

11. The handle (FIG. 7-17B) need not be the same wood as the rest of the board. A contrasting color is attractive. Having it thinner than the board makes it easier to grip. Well round the parts that will be held. Join it to the board with four, 1/4-inch dowels (FIG. 7-17C). Varnish or polish the handle, but leave the board plain or treat it with vegetable oil.

Hot pads

Ventilated wood kitchen hot pads can be made from offcuts, particularly those resulting from cutting pieces down to size on a table saw. These are thin and parallel, and too good to throw away. The pads described here are primarily intended for kitchen use, but they have other uses, too. One use can be under a plant pot. You could also use one on the dining table under a coffee pot. A gardener would be glad of some in a greenhouse.

Sizes depend on the available strips, but for the sake of the instructions it is assumed your pieces will make pads 6 inches or 7 inches square. You are unlikely to want them smaller, but you can use the same construction for pads up to twice as large.

Any wood can be used. Alternating woods of different colors produces a pleasing design. If hard and soft woods are mixed, the hardwoods should be put outside to better resist wear. Strips underneath can be a different color from those on top. For pads that will be used near food, avoid resinous, oily or aromatic woods. Light colors look hygienic, but darker woods are less likely to show burn marks from very hot pots.

12. The first pad (FIG. 7-18A) has strips glued and screwed from below. As an example, the wood is assumed to be 1/4 inch by 1 1/4 inch and 1/2 inch by 3/4 inch (FIG. 7-18B). Prepare the strips and lightly round the edges of the top pieces. Drill the lower pieces with deep countersinks so the screw heads finish below the surface. Choose thin screws that penetrate the top pieces far enough to grip, but not go through. Glue and screw the outer strips first. See that the assembly is square, then position the other pieces. Let the glue set, then plane the outer edges, round the corners and sand the surfaces and all exposed edges.

13. The second pad (FIG. 7-18C) is made similarly, but it has a border. Make the main part the same as the first pad, but leave the corners square and be careful to get the finished edges square to the surface. The border can be a thin one standing up a little (FIG. 7-18D), or it can be thicker and finished level (FIG. 7-18E). You have a choice of corners. Thin wood is best mitered (FIG. 7-18F), but the wider pieces can overlap (FIG. 7-18G). In this second method, you can produce an interesting effect by arranging the laps in turn around the pad, and you will also have the convenience of being able to trim ends after assembly. Border strips can be joined with glue only, if you have adequate clamping facilities, or a few pins set below the surface and covered with stopping can be used.

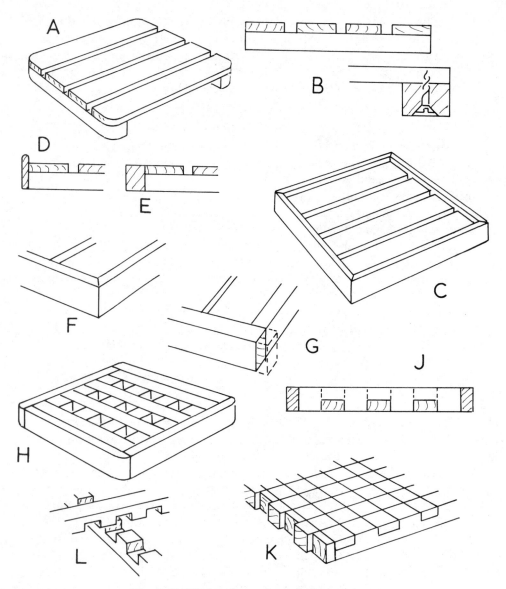

Fig. 7-18. Kitchen hot pads made from strips.

14. If your available strips are nearer a square section, you can cross them level, so the pad can be used either way. In the example, it is assumed the strips are ³/₄-inch by ³/₄-inch sections (FIG. 7-18H). The pieces cross with spaces the same width as the wood and there is a level thin border (FIG. 7-18J). Prepare the wood so all pieces are exactly the same section, or you will have difficulty with the joints. Mark across all the pieces together (FIG. 7-18K). Mark and cut the halved joints so surfaces will finish level

(FIG. 7-18L). Glue the pieces, then level the outer edges and add border strips, using one of the methods described for the previous example. Sand all over and round the outer edges and corners to produce an attractive pad.

15. For most purposes, these pads are best left untreated. A plant pot stand can be stained and polished or painted. A coffee pot stand can have a plain center with a polished border. A set of four or more identical pads are an attractive gift. Small ones might be used as coasters for a den or playroom.

8

Outdoor equipment

The earliest settlers had to provide creature comfort quickly with any wood to hand and often had few tools. Those crude pieces of furniture had to serve all their needs until they were more settled and could spend time fashioning more presentable long-lasting items, some of which survive today.

Many crude, temporary pieces of furniture had to be used indoors in the early days, but we can follow some of the designs to make furniture for the yard, patio and garden.

Wood in its natural form is the basis of most of these pieces of outdoor furniture. Some may keep the bark, but wood with loose bark should be stripped. Evidence of a chain saw can be avoided by cutting away the saw marks. Logs should be split or cleft, if possible, although it was not long before the pioneers set up saw mills and signs of saw marks on a bench or table surface are not wrong. Branches roughly tapered and driven into holes to make legs form strong structures, particularly if tightened with wedges.

There is the consideration of seasoning. If wood is used too soon after it is felled, this 'green' wood shrinks. In some assemblies that works to your advantage. A hole can close tighter on the part fitted through it. A possible problem will be the opening of cracks in drying, which were not apparent in the undried wood.

If you want the furniture to stay outdoors permanently, consider the effect of weather. Some woods, such as teak and some oaks, are naturally durable, but most woods should be treated with preservative. Ideally, the wood should be soaked in the preservative, but brushing on and repeating this treatment occasionally is acceptable.

Painting improves the appearance of some items, but do not expect paint to provide much protection against rot. Frequent painting may delay rot, but moisture gets through layers of paint.

If glue is used, it should be a waterproof type, such as a two-part boatbuilding glue. Apart from its strength, a closely glued joint does not admit water, and it is in open joints that first attacks of rot may occur.

Benches

Slab bench

A piece cut completely across a log can be made into a seat (FIG. 8-1A). It should be cut to one side of the pith center of the log, since that is weak. Thickness depends on size, but for a bench seat 5 feet long, it can be between $1^1/_2$ to 2 inches. Hardwood can be a little thinner than softwood.

**Materials List for
Slab Bench**

Natural wood $1^1/_2$ to 2 $\times$ 14 $\times$ 60
4 legs natural about 3 diameter $\times$ 24

If the outline has many pronounced irregularities, cut them level (FIG. 8-1B), but the uneven waney edge will be one of the features of the seat. Whether to remove bark or not depends on the wood. Pests gather under loose bark. If the bark shows signs of loosening, even in just a few parts, remove it all. In some woods the bark seems to be part of the wood and it should be left.

1. Cut the legs from natural poles, preferably of the same wood. Thickness is related to the size of the holes you can can drill—$1^1/_2$ inch diameter might be used for a bench. The peg legs can then be about 3 inches diameter. Remove loose bark.

   You do not need to be precise when setting the leg angles, but they should spread outward at about the same angle. A template can be made for a guide when drilling (FIG. 8-1C). With the underside of the slab narrower than the top, it is easier to get the legs correctly positioned if you drill from the underside. A small pilot drill can be used first to check the angle. If it is not exactly as you wish, the hole can be corrected when you enlarge it.
2. Arrange the legs a short distance in from the ends, but do not let the end of the slab extend far past the spread feet, or the seat might be unstable.
3. Start with the legs too long. Taper the ends to drive into the holes. It helps to draw a circle on the end of a size to match the hole, then work down to that (FIG. 8-1D).
4. Make a saw cut across the end of the leg. Drive in the leg so the cut is across the grain of the slab, then drive in a wedge (FIG. 8-1E). Cut the end level.

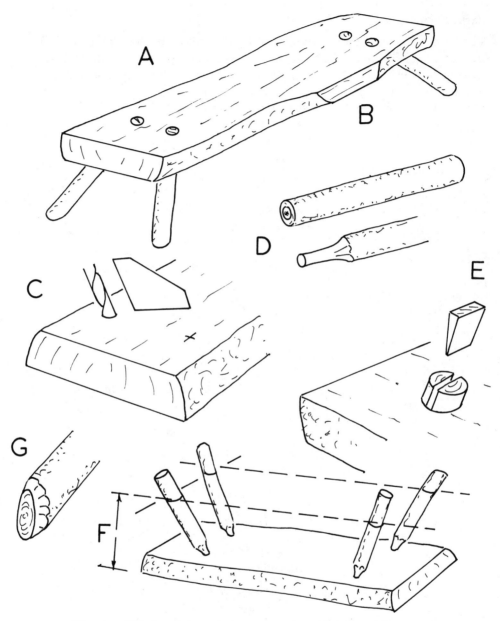

Fig. 8-1. *This bench is made from natural wood slabs and branches.*

5. When all four legs are fitted, invert the bench on a flat surface and measure the legs (FIG. 8-1F). If they are cut level at 16 inches, that should suit most situations. To minimize splintering, bevel the bottoms of the legs all around (FIG. 8-1G).

Slashed bench

A bench can be made from sawn boards, which also can be machine-planed, but the wood can be treated to give it a primitive appearance. This bench (FIG. 8-2) is made of parallel machined boards, but much of the straightness is broken up by irregular bevelling. The suggested sizes (FIG. 8-3) show fairly stout hardwood boards. You may have to adapt sizes to suit available wood.

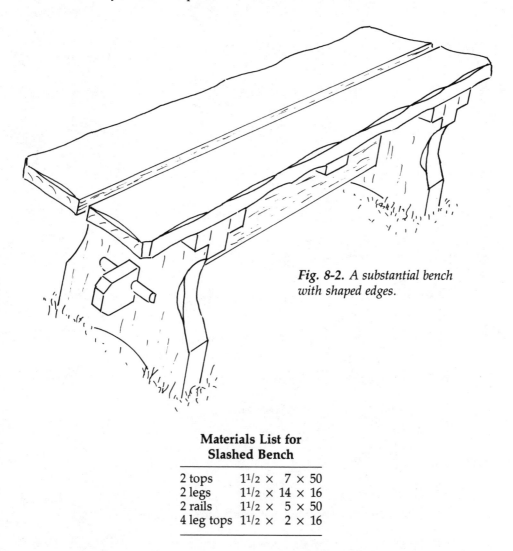

Fig. 8-2. *A substantial bench with shaped edges.*

Materials List for
Slashed Bench

2 tops	$1^{1}/_{2} \times 7 \times 50$
2 legs	$1^{1}/_{2} \times 14 \times 16$
2 rails	$1^{1}/_{2} \times 5 \times 50$
4 leg tops	$1^{1}/_{2} \times 2 \times 16$

1. Mark out the pair of legs (FIGS. 8-3B and 4A). Do not cut the mortise yet.
2. Make the bottom rail (FIG. 8-3C). Cut tenons on the ends (FIG. 8-4B), with plenty of length to resist the thrust of tightening the wedge on the end-grain.
3. Cut mortises in the legs to match the tenons.

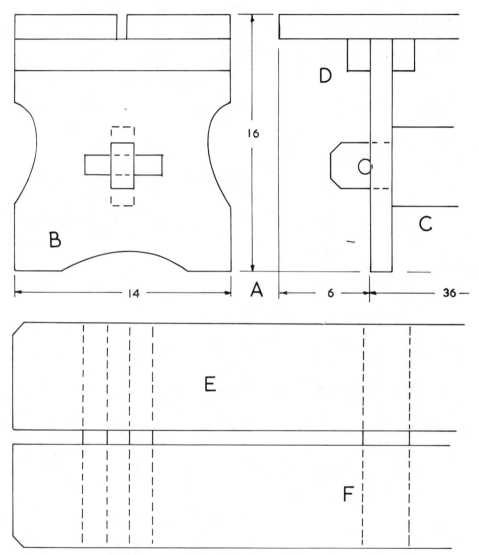

Fig. 8-3. Details of the bench with shaped edges.

4. Drill across the tenons so a small part of a hole is within the thickness of an end (FIG. 8-4C). Make the hole 1 inch diameter or larger.
5. Make pegs to drive through the holes. Cut them approximately round, and plane a taper so as a peg is driven, it presses against the leg and draws the tenon tight. If you cut the peg too long, you can experiment with the amount of taper, then cut off excess after assembly.
6. Thicken across the tops of the legs (FIG. 8-3D) with pieces nailed on.
7. Make the top from two boards (FIG. 8-3E). Allow for a gap of about 1/2 inch between them. This will help release rainwater.

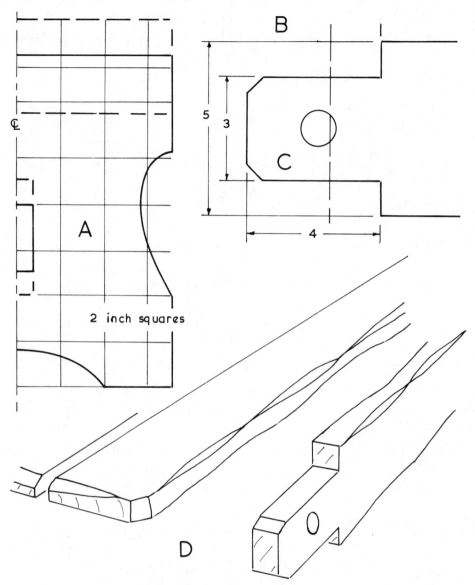

Fig. 8-4. Shaping of bench parts.

8. Before assembly, scallop around all the exposed edges so very little straight edges are left (FIG. 8-4D). Also do this around the leg edges and at the board ends. A drawknife may be used, but a broad chisel with its bevel downwards or a round-bottomed plane can also be used. Take sharpness off this slashing so there are no rough edges to scratch you or tear clothing.

9. Join the legs with the wedged bottom rail. Have the assembly standing on a flat surface. Check that the legs are upright. Nail on the seat boards.
10. To strengthen the top, invert the bench and nail a strip across under the center of the top boards (FIG. 8-3F).

Braced bench

When you sit on a chair or stool, weight spreads directly to the legs. When the greater length of a bench is sat on, the load is trying to bend the top between the legs, and this must be resisted. If the top is thick, its inherent stiffness will be enough, but otherwise rails under the top or diagonal bracing, as in this bench, must be used to resist the load (FIG. 8-5A).

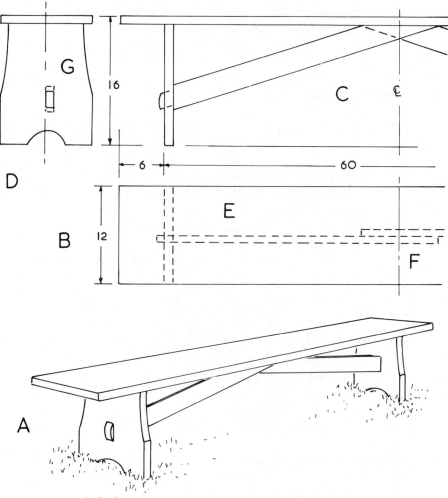

Fig. 8-5. This bench is braced with diagonal struts.

The bench should be made of hardwood at least 1¹/₂ inches thick. The sizes given (FIG. 8-5B) will produce a seat for three people, but you may adjust the sizes to suit your needs or the available material. Most of the joints are glued, so using planed wood is advisable because meeting sawn surfaces does not produce a tightly glued bond.

Materials List for
Braced Bench

1 top	1¹/₂ × 12 × 74
2 legs	1¹/₂ × 12 × 17
2 braces	1¹/₂ × 3 × 40

1. Set out the main lines of a front view (FIG. 8-5C) fullsize, showing the slopes of the two braces. Their centerlines should meet under the center of the top. This drawing shows what angles to cut ends and joints.
2. Mark out the two legs (FIG. 8-5D). The tops are 2 inches narrower than the seat, and there are 2 inch wide tenons (FIG. 8-6A). Shape the sides and bottom, but leave cutting the mortises until later.
3. Mark out the seat (FIG. 8-5E) and cut the mortises to match the tenons on the legs. Take sharpness off the edges and corners or fully round them.
4. Prepare the pieces for the two braces with some excess length at first. Use your setting to determine the lengths and angles at the overlap and where the braces should go though the legs.
5. At the legs, reduce the braces to 2 inches deep (FIG. 8-6B). Leave a little extra length at this stage.
6. At the other ends, cut long angles that fit under the seat.
7. As the meeting surfaces of the braces should be on the centerline of the bench (FIG. 8-5F), the mortises should be on opposite sides of the centerlines of the legs (FIG. 8-5G). With the tenons as guides to the angles, cut the mortises.
8. Enter the tenons in the mortises for a test assembly. Overlap the meeting braces and clamp them. Try the seat above this assembly. Make sure the seat mortises match the tenons, and that the shoulders of the leg tenons and the top surfaces of the meeting braces are level. Make adjustments, then glue and screw the overlapping braces. Round the ends of the braces that project through the legs, then glue them in place.
9. It is helpful to wedge the leg tenons, so make saw cuts across them before gluing them into the seat mortises. Drive in wedges (FIG. 8-6C) and plane off level.
10. Glue the overlaps of the braces under the seat and screw downwards into them. These can be counterbored screws with plugs glued over them.

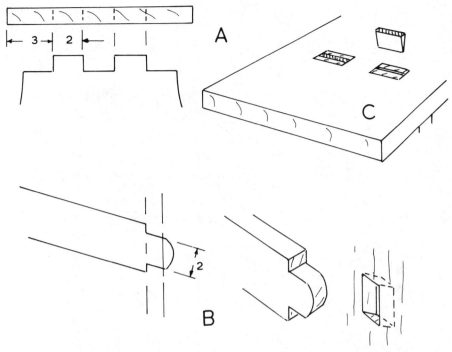

Fig. 8-6. *Joints of the bench with diagonal struts.*

Armchair

There is not a much simpler construction than using wood of all one section and nailing or screwing it together. This armchair is made throughout of wood in 1-inch by 4-inch finished sections and all the joints are glued and either nailed or screwed. Except for the joints at the rear ends of the arms, all the pieces merely overlap.

The armchair (FIG. 8-7) is a size that can be used outdoors as is, or it can have fitted cushions for seat and back. If made of suitable wood and treated with preservative, it can be left outside. If made of softwood and painted, it will be light enough to move under cover when not required.

The seat is 1 inch higher at the front than at the back. The two backrest strips are at an angle. The arms are parallel to the seat. Legs are vertical. You may find it worthwhile to draw the main lines of a side view fullsize to obtain the angle of the seat, but the angle is slight and you should be able to get the parts to fit correctly without doing this. Main sizes are shown in FIG. 8-8, but refer to FIG. 8-10 for details of some parts.

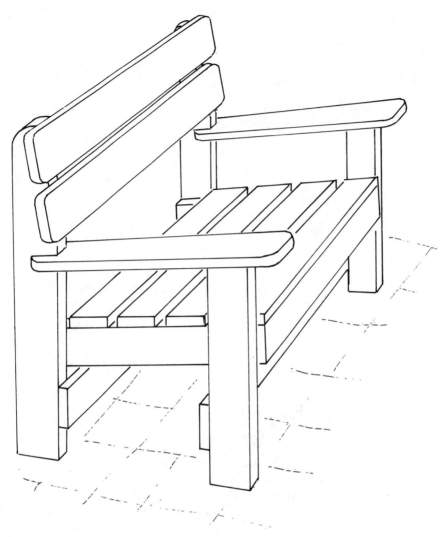

Fig. 8-7. This garden armchair is made with overlapping strips.

**Materials List
for Armchair**

(all 1 × 4
section)
2 rear legs   34
2 front legs   25
7 seat rails   24
2 back rails   26
2 lower rails   24
2 armrests   25

1. Make the two rear legs (FIGS. 8-9A and 10A). Mark on the positions of crossing parts. Round the rear top corners.
2. Make the two front legs (FIGS. 8-9B and 10B). Mark on the positions of crossing pieces. Note that the seat side is 1 inch higher on this than on the rear leg.
3. The seat front overlaps the seat sides (FIGS. 8-8A and 10C). Join it to the two sides and put on the four seat strips. The front one is level, then the oth-

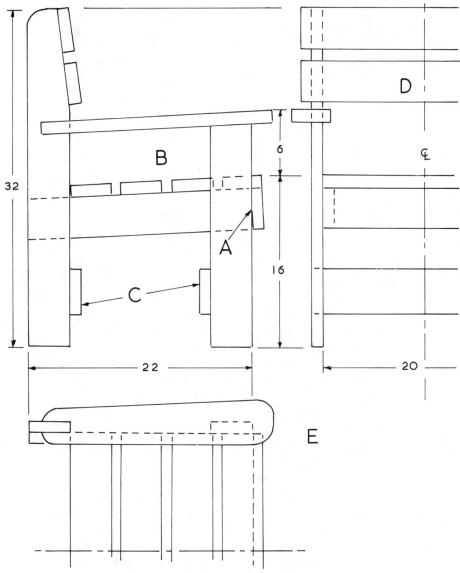

Fig. 8-8. Sizes of the armchair.

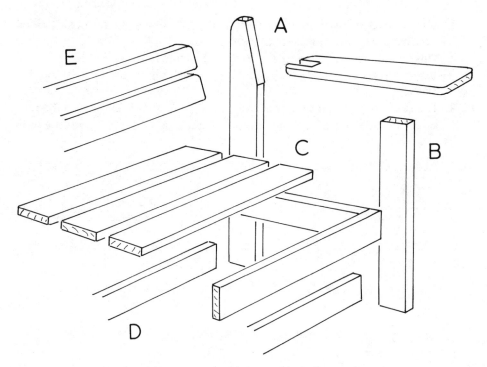

Fig. 8-9. *How parts of the armchair fit together.*

ers are spaced with about 1-inch gaps (FIGS. 8-8B, 9C and 10D), so the rear strip finishes against the rear legs.

4. Join the seat assembly to the legs at the marked heights. Use this assembly as a guide when making the other parts.

5. Fit the two lower rails (FIGS. 8-8C and 9D). As you nail or screw these on, check that the opposite legs are parallel.

6. Make the two back pieces (FIGS. 8-8D and 9E) so they overlap the legs by 1 inch. Round their outer corners and round the edges that will face forward. Delay fitting them until you make and fit the armrests.

7. The armrests can be left parallel, but they look better if you taper the outer edges to a 3-inch width at the back (FIGS. 8-8E and 10E).

8. Cut notches in the arms 3 inches deep so it fits around the rear legs. Round all the corners, and well round the edges that face upwards.

9. Try the arms in position. Arrange the arm notch heights on the rear legs so the back pieces can cross the legs above with the top piece level to the leg tops, and the bottom pieces immediately above the armrests, and a gap of 1 inch between them.

10. Fix these parts together. Even if you use nails in all the other crossings, you may consider it worthwhile for appearance sake to use counterbored and plugged screws through the arms into the tops of the front legs.

11. Make sure no nail or screw heads project. Remove any rough edges. Round parts that will be handled or come against clothing. Finish to suit the wood.

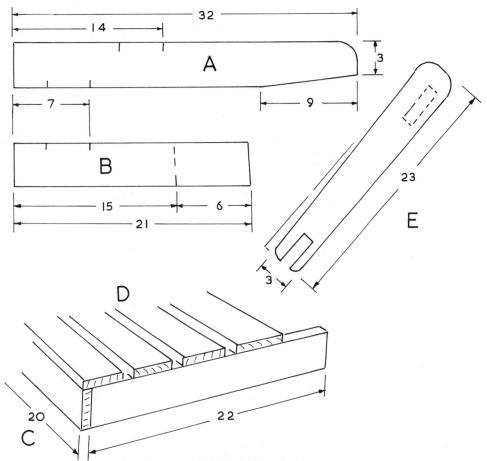

Fig. 8-10. Sizes of parts of the armchair.

Sawbuck Table

Tables with crossed legs were common in Early American furniture. Maybe the essential sawbuck was given a temporary top to form a table and the design grew from that. Such a table makes an attractive and useful piece of outdoor furniture. This one (FIG. 8-11) is large enough for meals for several people or for other purposes. Suggested sizes can vary (FIG. 8-12), but make sure the spread of feet is not less than the width of the top, preferably a little more. The given height is suitable for sitting and eating, comparable to an indoor dining table.

You could use hardwood or softwood. The design allows for common sections of wood.

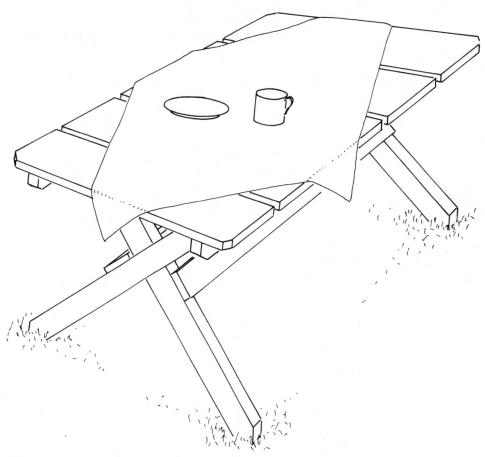

Fig. 8-11. This table has legs arranged in sawbuck manner.

**Materials List
for Sawbuck Table**

4 legs	2	× 4 ×	48
2 top rails	2	× 4 ×	56
2 bottom rails	1	× 6 ×	56
5 tops	$1^{1/4}$ × 9 ×		46

1. Set out the leg arrangements (FIG. 8-12A), starting with a fullsize drawing of the leg centerlines (FIG. 8-13A). From this draw the 4 inch widths of the wood and the cuts at tops and bottoms.
2. Using this drawing as a guide, cut the four legs. Mark their crossings to suit the actual widths of the wood.
3. Notch the crossings. Do not make full halving joints because that will weaken the legs. Notch each piece not more than one-quarter of its thick-

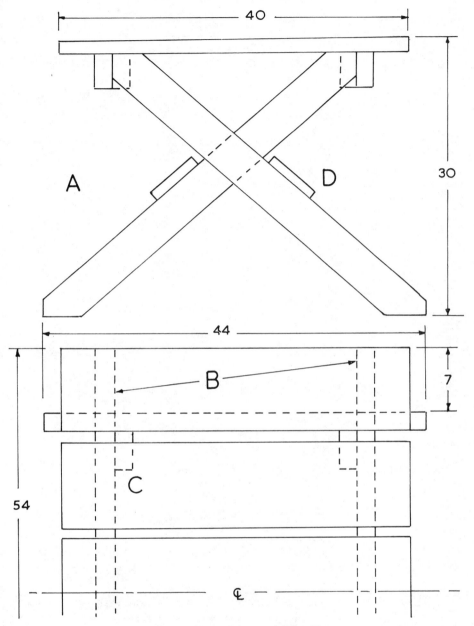

Fig. 8-12. *Sizes of the sawbuck table.*

ness (FIG. 8-13B). This is enough to prevent the legs from slipping out of position in relation to each other. Strength comes from glue and a 1/2-inch bolt through the center of each joint. Alternatively, nails or screws from both sides can be used.

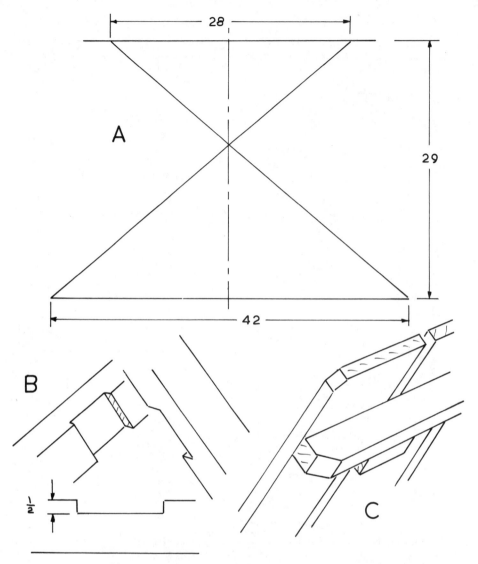

Fig. 8-13. Layout and joints of the sawbuck table.

4. The top is made of boards laid across. The individual width of the boards is not important, but the top is best made from fairly wide pieces. Draw them 9 inches wide. Allow for narrow gaps between them, to shed rainwater. Take the sharpness off all top edges and bevel the corners of the boards that will be at the ends.
5. Check the distance across the tops of the legs and space the rails under the top (FIG. 8-12B). Assemble the top with nails or screws into the rails. Check that the parts are square and parallel.

6. Put blocks inside the top rails to position the legs (FIGS. 8-12C and 13C). Allow for the different alignment of the legs.
7. Locate the legs against the blocks and nail them into the blocks and through the rails, using long nails through slightly undersize holes.
8. Support the assembly inverted, with the legs square to the top, while you nail on the lower rails (FIG. 8-12D).
9. Take the sharpness off exposed edges and complete the table with paint or preservative.

Permanent Table with Removable Top

Some early tables used outdoors had frameworks permanently set up, but the top was removable so it could be cleaned and stored out of the weather. This idea is just as good today, and this table is arranged with its framework set into the ground and a top that can be fitted securely or taken away for storage (FIG. 8-14).

The framework can be sawn wood, or an alternative, that uses rustic poles is suggested later. Sizes can be arranged to suit your needs, but those shown (FIG. 8-15A) make a table of useful height and area.

You must check the firmness of the ground. Legs should penetrate about 12 inches. In some soil you can point and drive the legs in, but elsewhere you might have to dig holes and pack soil around the legs. Reasonable rigidity is important, but the bracing will help provide mutual support between the legs.

Materials List for Permanent Table with Removable Top			
4 legs	$2^{1}/_{2}$ ×	$2^{1}/_{2}$ ×	42
2 end rails	1 ×	4 ×	30
2 side rails	1 ×	4 ×	50

1. Cut four legs (FIG. 8-15B). Bevel around the tops. Allow for the tops of the legs finishing $3/4$ inch above the surface of the table top, then mark the legs in pairs for the rail notches (FIG. 8-15C). Cut the notches $1/2$ inch deep to match the rails. These provide location and security, but strength comes from a $1/2$ inch bolt through the middle of each joint.
2. Make the two crosswise rails (FIG. 8-15D) project $1^{1}/_{2}$ inches from the legs.
3. Make the lengthwise rails so the ends are level with the legs (FIG. 8-15E).
4. Use the rail sizes as guides to space the legs in the ground. Set the legs so they are upright and the tops are at the same level. A spirit level on a straight board will ensure accuracy.
5. Position the rails between the legs and bolt them in place.
6. Measure the framework to get the sizes for the table top. Allow this to fit easily—there can be up to $1/2$ inch of clearance.

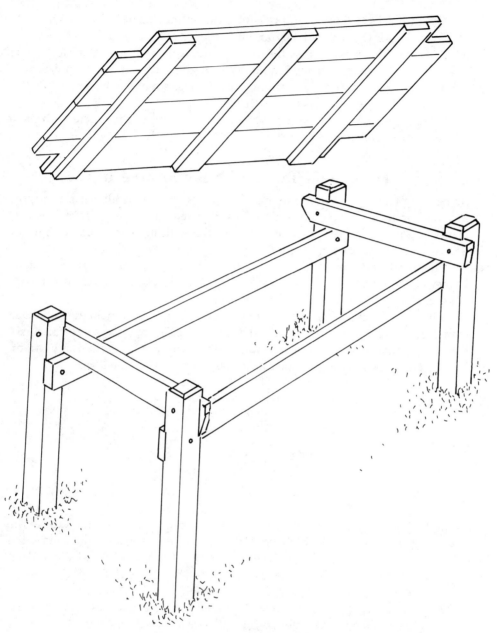

Fig. 8-14. *Structure for a permanent table with a lift-off top.*

7. You can make the table top from any convenient number of boards, but four are shown. The top should be as wide as the lengths of the cross rails or a little more. It should be long enough to extend 1 inch past the legs at each end.

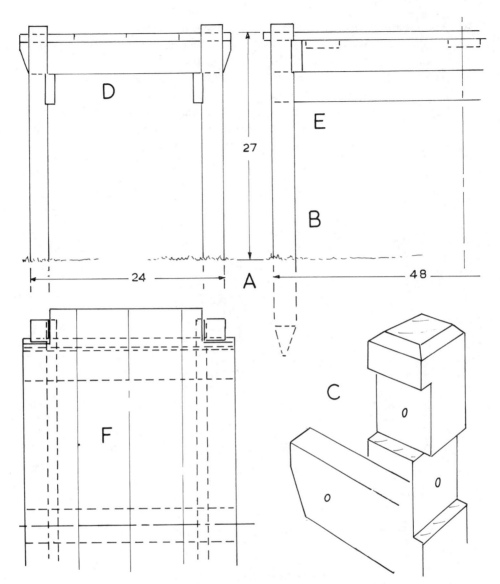

Fig. 8-15. Parts of a permanent table using squared wood.

8. Assemble the top with three crossbars (FIGS. 8-14 and 15F). Use waterproof glue and nails or screws. Bevel exposed edges and remove sharpness or raggedness in the top parts. Even if other parts have sawn surfaces, you may wish to have a planed top surface.
9. Try the top in position. Protect the framework with preservative or paint. The top could be painted or left untreated so it can be scrubbed occasionally.

10. If you want to give a more rural appearance, the framework can be made of natural poles. They might be about 3 inch diameter for the legs and about 2 inch diameter for the horizontal parts.

11. As crossing poles do not provide the same stiffness given by flat notched pieces, allow for two horizontal poles each way (FIG. 8-16A). Hollow the legs for the other poles (FIG. 8-16B), but do not cut away so much that the legs are weakened. V grooves are easier to cut (FIG. 8-16C), and almost as strong as fitted curved hollows. Join the parts with central bolts.

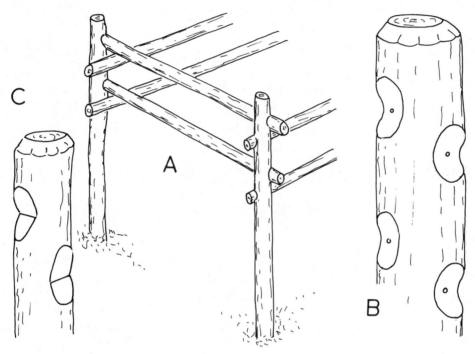

Fig. 8-16. Framework for a table made from natural poles.

Garden Tool Box

In the days when people baked bread at home, often in large batches, they allowed the dough to rise in a roomy box with tapered ends. Because of the weight, frequently handles were installed so two people could move the box where required. We do not have that need, but a similar and slightly bigger box is useful in a large garden for moving and storing tools.

This garden tool box should be large enough for many garden tools (FIG. 8-17), but it can be made to suit your needs. Keep the handles about 15 inches apart for easy handling. If the box is made about 17 inches high, it can serve as a seat when you want to rest from your labors and watch things grow. The sloping ends give leg clearance when you are walking and carrying the box.

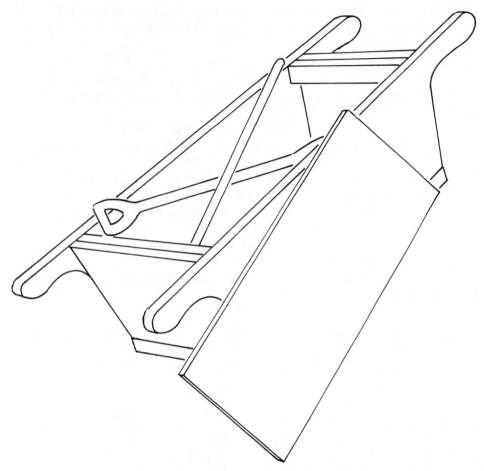

Fig. 8-17. This garden tool box is made to be carried by two people.

Use the full width of a board, if possible, and the grain at the ends should be vertical. You can nail two boards to them to make up each side without risk of joints failing. Similarly, the bottom can be made of two boards nailed in place. If necessary, in both cases, stiffening battens can be placed centrally across.

**Materials List
for Garden Tool Box**

2 sides	1 × 14 × 74
2 ends	1 × 13 × 16
4 end strips	1 × 2 × 15
1 bottom	1 × 13 × 50
1 lid	1 × 17 × 60

1. Mark out the two sides (FIG. 8-18A). Shape the handles to be $1^1/2$ inches deep at the thinnest part (FIG. 8-18B). If the grips are well-rounded that should suit most hands.
2. Make the two ends (FIGS. 8-18C and 19A) with the grain upright. Put a strip across each top and bevel the two edges to suit the slope of the end.
3. Put another strip across, near the bottom, leaving a sufficient gap for the box bottom (FIGS. 8-18D and 19B).
4. Make the bottom. Nail one box side to the two box ends and the bottom. If necessary, level the edges that will come against the second side, then nail that on.
5. Make the lid so it overhangs 1 inch all around. Put battens across (FIG. 8-19C), far enough in from the ends to locate the lid when put in place. If you make the lid from two or more boards, put a similar batten across the center to prevent warping.
6. It is advisable to raise the bottom off the ground, so nail 2-inch square strips under the ends (FIG. 8-18E).
7. You can treat the box with preservative or paint if you do not want to leave it untreated.

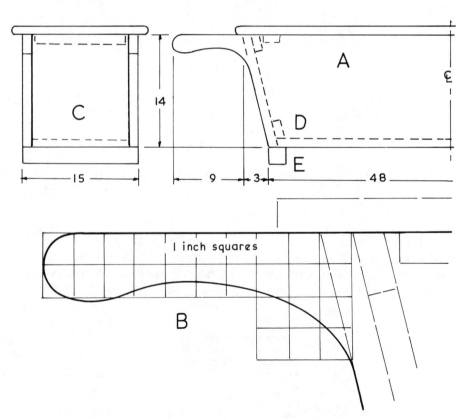

Fig. 8-18. Sizes and handle shape for a garden tool box.

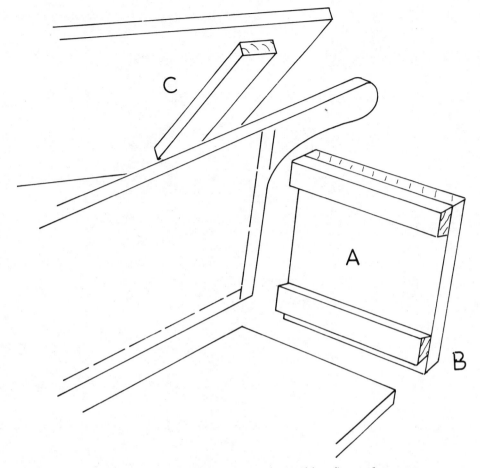

Fig. 8-19. How parts of the garden tool box fit together.

Index

A

armchair, outdoor type, 187-191
authenticity in reproduction pieces, 2

B

benches
    box-type, 11-15
    braced bench, outdoor-type, 185
    slab bench, outdoor-type, 180-181
    slashed bench, outdoor-type, 182-185
    storage-type workbench, 150-154
    wagon-seat bench, 37-40
bins, stackable, 55-58
block of shelves, wall-hung, 72-77
book trough, two-tiered, 106-109
box bench, 11-15
boxes
    box bench, 11-15
    carrying boxes, 41-47
    dadoed box with tray, 51-55
    garden tool box, 198-201
    hanging boxes, 65-72
braced bench, outdoor-type, 185-187
butcherblock kitchen blocks, 173-175

C

cabinets
    small-sized cabinet, 145-150
    storage bench, 150-154

storage cabinet, 141-145
    wall-hung, 77-82
caddy, wall-hung, 90-95
carrier/magazine rack, 155-159
carrying stack-boxes, 41-47
chairs
    peasant chair, 21-26
    rush-seated chair, 28-36
chests, pioneer chest, 47-51
coat-rack, Shaker-style, 82-86
containers, 41-63
    carrying stack-boxes, 41-47
    dado box with tray, 52-55
    desk with lid, 58-63
    garden tool box, 198-201
    hanging boxes, 65-72
    pioneer chest, 47-51
    stacking bins, 55-58
corner stand or whatnot, 109-113
counterboring for screws, 4-5
cutting boards, 171

D

dado box with tray, 51-55
dado joints, 5-7
desk tidy, rotating, 167-170
desk, 58-63
display rack, 113-118
dovetailed joints, 7-9
doweled joints, 5

drying frame or towel rack, 159-162
drying rack, 97-101

F

fasteners, 2, 4-5
frame, mirror or picture, 86-90

G

garden tool box, 198-201
glues, 2

H

half-lap or halving joints, 5-6
hanging boxes, 65-72
hanging cabinet, 77-82
hanging caddy, 90-95
hanging furniture, 65-95
  coat-rack, Shaker-style, 82-86
  hanging boxes, 65-72
  hanging cabinet, 77-82
  hanging caddy, 90-95
  mirror or picture frame, 86-90
  shelf block, 72-77
hardware, 2
hinges, 2
hot pads, 175-177

J

joints, 5-9

K

kitchen boards, 171

L

lathe-turned stand, 118-120
library stool, 26-28

M

magazine rack, 155-159
Mayflower stool with drawer, 15-21
mirror, 86-90
mortise-and-tenon joints, 7-8

N

nails, 4

O

outdoor equipment, 179-201
  armchair, 187-191
  braced bench, 185-187
  garden tool box, 198-201
  permanent table with removable top,
    195-198

sawbuck table, 191-195
slab bench, 180-181
slashed bench, 182-185

P

panels, 1
peasant chair, 21-26
permanent table with removable top,
  195-198
picture frame, 86-90
pioneer chest, 47-51
planing, 3-4
plans and layout, 3
plant stand, 101-105
plugging counterbored holes, 4-5
plywood and particleboard, 2

Q

quilt rack, 97-101

R

racks and stands, 97-120
  book trough, two-tiered, 106-109
  carrier/magazine rack, 155-159
  coat-rack, Shaker-style, 82-86
  corner stand or whatnot, 109-113
  display rack, 113-118
  drying frame or towel rack, 159-162
  drying rack, 97-101
  plant stand, 101-105
  quilt rack, 97-101
  turned stand, 118-120
railed table, 137-141
reproduction pieces, 2
rotating desk tidy, 167-170
rush-seated chair, 28-36

S

sanding, 3-4
sawbuck table, 191-195
scraping, 3-4
screws, 4-5
seating projects, 11-40
  box bench, 11-15
  library stool, 26-28
  Mayflower stool with drawer, 15-21
  peasant chair, 21-26
  rush-woven chair, 28-36
  wagon seat bench, 37-40
Shaker style coat-rack, 82-86
shelves, shelf block, wall-hung, 72-77
slab bench, outdoor-type, 180-181
slab table, 121-127
slashed bench, outdoor-type, 182-185

small-sized cabinet, 145-150
stacked carrying boxes, 41-47
stacking bins, 55-58
standard tables, 127-137
steps, 162-167
stools
   library stool, 26-28
   Mayflower stool with drawer, 15-21
storage bench, 150-154
storage cabinet, 141-145
surfacing techniques, 3-4

T

tables
   permanent table with removable top,
     195-198
   railed table, 137-141
   sawbuck table, outdoor-type, 191-195
   slab table, 121-127
   standard tables, 127-137
tenoned joints, 7-8
towel rack, 159-162
turned stand, 118-120

two-tiered book trough, 106-109

U

utility items, 155-177
   butcherblock construction kitchen
     boards, 173-175
   carrier/magazine rack, 155-159
   desk tidy, rotating, 167-170
   drying frame or towel rack, 159-162
   hot pads, 175-177
   kitchen cutting boards, 171
   steps, 162-167

V

veneers, 1

W

wagonseat bench, 37-40
whatnot corner stand, 109-113
wood selection and use, 1, 150-154
   dry vs. green wood, 179
   protection from elements, 179-180

Other Bestsellers of Related Interest

COUNTRY ELEGANCE: Projects for Woodworkers
—Edward A. Baldwin

Add a cozy country mood to your home with this one-of-a-kind collection of challenging and rewarding project plans that you're sure to like—no matter what your skill level! This book presents step-by-step, illustrated instructions for 29 original country furniture designs for every room in your home. Projects are as practical as they are attractive, and range in difficulty from a small door harp to a deacon's bench and chest combination. 256 pages, illustrated. Book No. 3768, $14.95 paperback, $26.95 hardcover.

PUZZLES, BOXES AND TOYS:
Creative Scroll Saw Patterns—Percy W. Blandford

In this book, a master craftsman explores the surprisingly diverse uses for the scroll saw. Here you'll find an assortment of project plans—ranging from simple toys and outdoor ornaments to elaborate tables and cabinets—that take advantage of the scroll saw's capability for piercing wood and making intricate cuts. Most plans are suitable for beginners with a basic set of tools, while some are designed to challenge more experienced woodworkers. Each project includes a drawing of the finished piece, patterns, step-by-step assembly instructions, and a materials list. 224 pages, 158 illustrations. Book No. 3706, $12.95 paperback, $19.95 hardcover.

ONE-WEEKEND COUNTRY FURNITURE PROJECTS—Percy W. Blandford

Transform simple materials into beautiful, functional objects with this brand-new selection of original projects to use in and around your home, in an easy, one-weekend format, especially for time-conscious hobbyists. A basic understanding of woodworking techniques is all you need to build an attractive, durable piece of furniture in as little as 12 hours. You get nearly 50 original project plans—all requiring only simple hand tools and inexpensive materials—and ample drawings and instructions for every design. 240 pages, 163 illustrations. Book No. 3702, $14.95 paperback, $24.95 hardcover.

THE DRILL PRESS BOOK: Including 80 Jigs and Accessories to Make—R.J. DeCristoforo

The drill press, after the table saw, is the second most important tool in the workshop. In this well-illustrated guide, you'll discover unique ways to develop the tool's potential in over 80 project plans. As De Cristoforo guides you through each application of this versatile tool, you'll benefit from hundreds of hints based on his years of woodworking experience. 304 pages, 406 illustrations. Book No. 3609, $16.95 paperback, $25.95 hardcover.

GIFTS FROM THE WOODSHOP
—R.J. DeCristoforo

Whether you're a master craftsman or novice woodbutcher, you'll find something challenging in this collection of practical and attractive gift projects. You'll find instructions for building kitchen aids, plant hangers and stands, wind chimes, bird houses and feeders, toys, picture and mirror frames, shelves and racks, decorative plaques, and much more. All projects can be made using basic hand tools. 240 pages, 290 illustrations. Book No. 3591, $15.95 paperback, $24.95 hardcover.

DECKS AND PATIOS: Designing and Building Outdoor Living Spaces—Edward A. Baldwin

This handsome book will show you step-by-step how to take advantage of outdoor space. It's a comprehensive guide to designing and building decks and patios that fit the style of your home and the space available. You'll find coverage of a variety of decks, patios, walkways, and stairs. Baldwin helps you design your outdoor project, and then shows you how to accomplish every step from site preparation through finishing and preserving your work to ensure many years of enjoyment. 152 pages, 180 illustrations. Book No. 3326, $16.95 paperback, $26.95 hardcover.

RIP-OFF TIP-OFFS: Winning the Auto Repair Game—Robert Sikorsky

Don't get ripped off when you take your car for repairs. This book gives you the ammunition to stop repair scams before they start. Sikorsky exposes popular tactics used by cheats and describes how to ensure a fair deal. If you have been ripped off, he tells you how to complain effectively—both to get your money back and to put the charlatans out of business for good. But most importantly, Sikorsky tells how to avoid getting burned in the first place by learning how your car works and by keeping it in good condition. 140 pages, 29 illustrations. Book No. 3572, $9.95 paperback, $16.95 hardcover.

THE WONDERFUL WORLD OF WHIRLIGIGS & WIND MACHINES: 15 Projects
—Alan and Gill Bridgewater

Here are complete instructions for wind-operated sculptures. Projects include: a New England soldier whirligig, a Dutch windmill weathervane, a pecking bird whirligig, and a fisherman windmill. You get working drawings with grids for sizing, detailing, cutting, and painting, plus illustrated step-by-step instructions. You'll develop and test your woodworking skills using a scroll saw, coping saw, hand drill, woodcarving tools, turning chisels, and lathe. 208 pages, 192 illustrations. Book No. 3349, $12.95 paperback, $21.95 hardcover.

Prices Subject to Change Without Notice.

Look for These and Other TAB Books at Your Local Bookstore

To Order Call Toll Free 1-800-822-8158
(in PA, AK, and Canada call 717-794-2191)

or write to TAB Books, Blue Ridge Summit, PA 17294-0840.

Title	Product No.	Quantity	Price

☐ Check or money order made payable to TAB Books

Charge my ☐ VISA ☐ MasterCard ☐ American Express

Acct. No. _____ Exp. _____

Signature: _____

Name: _____

Address: _____

City: _____

State: _____ Zip: _____

Subtotal $ _____

Postage and Handling
($3.00 in U.S., $5.00 outside U.S.) $ _____

Add applicable state and local
sales tax $ _____

TOTAL $ _____

TAB Books catalog free with purchase; otherwise send $1.00 in check or money order and receive $1.00 credit on your next purchase.

Orders outside U.S. must pay with international money order in U.S. dollars.

TAB Guarantee: If for any reason you are not satisfied with the book(s) you order, simply return it (them) within 15 days and receive a full refund.   **BC**